Chen Tai Chi

Traditional Instructions
from the Chen Village

Volume 1

An Anthology of Articles from the *Journal of Asian Martial Arts*

Edited by Michael A. DeMarco, M.A.

Copyright © 2015 by
Via Media Publishing Company
941 Calle Mejia #822
Santa Fe, NM 87501 USA
E-mail: md@goviamedia.com

All articles in this anthology were originally published in the *Journal of Asian Martial Arts*. Listed according to the table of contents for this anthology:

Book and cover design by Via Media Publishing Company
Edited by Michael A. DeMarco, M.A.

Cover illustration
Illustration by Patricia Sadiq • http://eyedoodles.com
Courtesy of Stephen Berwick • http://truetaichi.com

ISBN: 978-1-893765-08-5

www.viamediapublishing.com

contents

preface

When we think of martial arts in "old China," we get visions of violent convulsions of dynastic change, devastating rebellions, civil wars, and banditry. Throughout the centuries there was a need for masters who possessed highly effective martial skills for positions in the military, protection services, and law enforcement. Out of this historical reality emerged a national treasure we call taijiquan.

Chen-style taijiquan formulated during the days of military strategist Qi Jiguang (1528–1587), and its founder is considered to be militia battalion commander Chen Wangting (1600–1680). The art evolved. Its mystique remains fundamentally a true fighting art, including bare-handed forms and applications, plus an arsenal of weapons that includes the spear, straight sword, broadsword, and halberd. Then there are the associated training methods used to master this complete system, such as qigong, push-hands, and standing post. All of these practices are infused with knowledge associated with the physical and mental aspects of the human condition.

Chen style encompasses a complete martial system. It has a deserved reputation for its combative efficiency, but also as a health-nurturing modality. The vastness of the Chen-style curriculum is way beyond the scope of most people to fully learn, so practitioners focus on what they can handle. Usually a solo routine is sufficient. Since all taiji styles stem from the original Chen family system, the Chens certainly share in the credit for taiji's popularity in general, especially as an exercise purely for health benefits.

Regardless of taiji style—be it Chen, Yang, Wu, Sun, Hao, or other—any serious taiji practitioner or scholar should have some understanding of the Chen family roots to get a vision of the whole tree. This two-volume anthology brings much of the rich heritage conveniently together for your reading. In this first volume, prepare yourself to sit at the feet of the main representatives of the Chen Village, including Chen Xiaowang, Chen Xiaoxing, and Wang Xi'an. Read rare text from Chen Xin, a member of the literati who expounded on the inner workings of Chen taiji by utilizing Daoist and traditional medical knowledge.

In addition to the detailed history and penetrating philosophy you'll find here, perhaps of greater importance are the clear explanations outlining each step in the learning process toward mastering Chen-style taiji. Only a very high-level teacher can understand what methods of instruction work best. Students don't know; that's why they should follow a teacher's instructions as closely as possible. Chapters included here clarify what proper training entails and why much time and effort (*gongfu*) are necessary to gain results. As echoed among practitioners in taiji's birthplace: "If you drink water from Chen Village, your feet know how to kick." This two-volume edition brings you to the village for traditional instruction.

Michael A. DeMarco
Santa Fe, NM
August 2015

author bio notes

Stephan Berwick, M.A., has a Chinese martial arts background spanning over thirty years. Bow Sim Mark was his early mentor. He went on to work for martial arts Hong Kong film director Yuen Wo Ping. Upon returning to the U.S., Mr. Berwick began intensive Chen taiji training under the celebrated Chen Stylist, Ren Guangyi, and also closely mentored by top members of taiji's founding family, the Chens of Chenjiagou. Mr. Berwick holds an M.A. in International Law from the Fletcher School of Law and Diplomacy, Tufts University in cooperation with Harvard University.

Asr Cordes has studied martial arts since the age of eight and has focused on internal martial arts training since 1992. He is a senior student of Cheng Jincai, a twentieth-generation representative of Chen-style taijiquan. Asr Cordes currently is a professional Chen-style taijiquan instructor, international gold medalist, and freelance martial arts writer.

Michael DeMarco, M.A., founder of the *Journal of Asian Martial Arts*, received his degree from Seton Hall University's Department of Asian Studies. In 1964 he began his martial arts study in Indonesian kuntao-silat; since 1973 he has focused on taijiquan. Mr. DeMarco studied under Yang Qingyu (d. 2002) in Taiwan, in the Yang-style lineage of Xiong Yonghe (1886–1981). He also studied Chen style in Taiwan under Tu Zongren and Du Yuze (1886–1990), in the lineage of Chen Yanxi.

David Gaffney, B.A., received a bachelor's degree in leisure and human communication from Manchester University, England. He has been training in the Asian martial arts since 1980 and received his instructor's certificate from the Wenxian Chen Taiji Research and Promotion Center in 1997. He holds a fifth-degree grade with the Chinese Wushu Association. Mr. Gaffney has made numerous trips to the Far East to train with some of the leading figures of Chen taiji, including Chen Xiaowang, Chen Zhenglei, Chen Xiaoxing, Zhu Tiancai, and Wang Haijun. With Davidine Siaw-Voon Sim he is the coauthor of *Chen Style Taijiquan: The Source of Taiji Boxing* (North Atlantic Books).

Miriam O'Conner, M.A., has been practicing taijiquan in the Zheng Manqing (Cheng Man-ch'ing) lineage during the last decade. She holds an M.A. degree in languages and literature from the University of Auckland (New Zealand) and a master of Chinese from the Université de Provence (Aix-Marseille III). O'Connor taught languages at the University of Auckland and the Cultural University in Taiwan. Currently she is lecturing in French at Temasek Polytechnic in Singapore.

Dietmar Stubenbaum is the president and cofounder of the German branch of the International Society of Chen Taijiquan. He studied Chen style in Taiwan under Tu Zongren in the lineage of Du Yuze. He became a student of Chen Peishan and Chen Peiju (lineage of Chen Lixian and Chen Liqing) to focus on the small frame (xiaojia) style. He received a teaching certificate from the National Taijiquan Association of the Republic of China. Master Stubenbaum teaches in Friedrichafen, Germany. www.die-pagode.de

Wong, Jiaxiang was born in 1925 in Heilongjiang province and later moved to Taiwan. He studied many forms of Daoist exercise in addition to taijiquan. In Taiwan he became the leading disciple of Chen-style master Du Yuze, from whom he learned the old frame and new frame. He has lived and taught for many years in Tainan city. As a leading scholar of taijiquan, he has numerous publications on Yang, Sun, Wu, Hao, Lee, and Chen styles.

Chenjiagou:
The History of the Taiji Village

by David Gaffney, B.A.

Memorial to Chen Bu –
Patriarch of the Chen family
and founder of Chenjiagou.
All photographs courtesy of David Gaffney.

Introduction

Chenjiagou (Chen Family Ditch), alongside the Shaolin Temple and Wudang Mountain, is one of the most significant martial arts locations in China and is often referred to simply as the "Taiji Village." It is located in Henan Province, central China, and is surrounded by four large cities: Xinxiang to the east, Zhengzhou to the south, Luoyang to the west, and Jiaozuo to the north. An examination of Chenjiagou's history shows how difficult it has been for the village to preserve its legacy. A combination of political, social, and environmental factors has conspired to challenge taijiquan's very survival in its birthplace.

Traditional Community

To chart the experience of generations of taijiquan practitioners in Chenjiagou in any kind of meaningful way, one must consider how they perceived the world. To Western eyes, Chenjiagou, like many remote rural communities throughout the world, seems to give off a sense of timeless permanence. Each generation of the Chen clan preserved and built upon the family art passed down to

1

them. In *Understanding Folk Religion*, the author captures this sense: "Emphasis on membership in a greater family provides people with a strong sense of identity. Including ancestors provides a sense of stability and continuity" (Heibert, 1999: 179). Ancestor worship served to strengthen ties of kinship to the extent that within traditional Chinese social organization, the concept of the patrilineal family is taken to be the essential cohesive unit in society. Blood kinship is unquestionably the social tie of greatest significance (Hucker, 1975: 57).

Chen Bu's Journey to Chenjiagou

While taijiquan was widely acknowledged to be created in the late 17th century, the Chenjiagou villagers trace their ancestry back to Chen Bu, the historical patriarch of the Chen clan. Chen Bu founded the village during the turbulent early years of the Ming Dynasty (1368–1644). It was a time of war, devastation, and chaos as the previous Yuan Dynasty (1271–1368) was coming to an end. Law and order were non-existent and the population lived in poverty and fear. The warrior Zhu Yuanzhang emerged victorious and took control of China, establishing the Ming Dynasty.

During a raid in Huaiqing Prefecture (today's Qinyang city, which in those days governed eight counties, including Wen County where Chenjiagou is located), Zhu Yuanzhang's men were met with fierce resistance by Yuan General Tien Moer and sustained huge casualties. However, a single prefecture could not hold off sustained attacks from Zhu's vast army. It was finally defeated by lack of supplies and reinforcements, and the few remaining Yuan soldiers dispersed (Chen, 2004: 1).

The consequences for the region were catastrophic. "After Zhu Yuanzhang ascended the throne, he turned his anger on the common people of Huaiqing Prefecture, accusing them of helping the resistance against the imperial soldiers. He sent his solders to 'clean' Huaiqing three times by slaying all the innocent people. It is said that after the Ming soldiers finished pillaging a place, they often placed money, food, cloths, etc. at the crossroad in the center of a village. If these items were picked up, a new search would ensue. Although people went into hiding with their families, eight to nine out of ten did not manage to escape the massacre. After the three 'cleansings' of the prefecture and its eight counties, an area of several thousand square kilometers were littered with blood and bodies. Almost no crops could be seen and not a single rooster could be heard in the thousand villages" (Chen, 2004: 1).

Records of the period tell of the implementation of a policy of mass migration and wasteland reclamation. A migration office was established in Shanxi Province, and local inhabitants were compelled to relocate to sparsely populated areas devastated by the war (one of which was Huaiqing Prefecture). One of those forced to move was Chen Bu. According to Chen Xiaowang, Chen Bu "originated from Dongtuhe Village, Hezhou (today's Jincheng County), Shanxi. In the first year of Hongwu [1367], Chen Bu with his whole family fled from famine to Hongdong. In the fifth year of Hongwu (1372), he was among the ones who were forced by government officials to move to Henan's Huaiqing Prefecture" (Chen, X., 2004: 1).

Since the traditional starting point for all migrations was beneath a scholar tree (*huaishu, sophora sinensis*), the saying persists today that the Chen family ancestors came from "Shanxi Hongdong Big Scholar Tree" (Gaffney & Sim, 2002: 10).

Chen Bu settled on a wide fertile flood plain in southeastern Huaiqing Prefecture, with the Yellow River (*Huanghe*) to the south and the Taihang Mountains to the north. A village was gradually established that was named Chen Bu's Village (*Chen Bu Zhuang*). The village bears his name to this day, though it is now part of Wen County instead of Qinyang.

The village, however, proved less than ideal as it was on low lying ground and prone to flooding. Chen Bu moved about five kilometers to the east, to Green Wind Ridge (*Qing Feng Ling*). The new place was named Chang Yang Village after a temple there. Chen Bu soon led an attack to destroy a nearby bandit stronghold that had been terrorizing the area. Chen Bu's reputation grew and he established a martial arts school to train the villagers.

Despite his many heroic exploits, the way the village eventually acquired its name is somewhat prosaic. "Areas on both sides of the Yellow River were frequently flooded. Many failed attempts were made to deepen the river. Parallel drainage ditches, therefore, were created to help deal with floodwaters. These came to be associated with families. Chen Bu's family name gave Chang Yang Village its modern name of Chenjiagou, meaning 'Chen Family Ditch'" (Gaffney & Sim, 2002).

The "Scholar Tree" in Shanxi province from which
Chen Bu began his migration to Henan Province.
Right, statue of taijiquan creator Chen Wangting.

3

The Birth of Taijiquan

While the art of taijiquan had yet to make an appearance, the Chen clan's martial tradition continued. It seems likely that the martial art practiced was external in nature. "The close proximity of the village to the Shaolin Temple gives credence to the theory that it may have been some form of Shaolin boxing. The Chen family was famous for several generations for their Cannon Fist Boxing (*Paochuiquan*) and was known as the Paochui Chen Family (*Paohcui Chen Jia*) (Gaffney & Sim, 2002: 10–11).

Detailed historical records of people, events, and martial arts started from the time of Chen Wangting (1600–1680). According to *Annals of Huaiqing Prefecture*, *Wen County Annals*, and *Anping County Annals*, in 1641, before the fall of the Ming Dynasty, Chen Wangting was a military officer and was commander of the Wen County garrison force. *The Genealogy of Chen Families* states that at the end of the Ming Dynasty, Chen Wangting was already famous for his martial skills, "having once defeated more than 1000 bandits and was a born warrior, as can be proven by the sword he used in combat" (Gaffney & Sim, 2002: 12).

Some three centuries earlier, Emperor Hongwu (imperial name of Ming Dynasty founder Zhu Yuanzhang) had established a powerful military machine with a million-man standing army. This was divided into basic garrison units (*wei*) of roughly five thousand men that were further subdivided into smaller companies (*so*). For major campaigns, soldiers were assembled from *wei* and *so* from the four corners of the country under the instruction of commanders from the capital. By Chen Wangting's time, however, the *wei-so* system had become a bureaucratic nightmare.

"The *wei–so* standing army declined in strength and fighting ability. It was supplemented by local militiamen, then by conscripts from the general population, and finally in the last Ming century by recruited mercenaries in awesome numbers. In the last Ming decades the military rolls swelled to a reported total of four million men. But they were poorly equipped, ill trained, and irregularly fed and clothed; only a small fraction of the total can have been effective soldiers" (Hucker, 1975: 327).

Chen Wangting was fiercely loyal to the Ming Dynasty and its fall ended any ambitions of advancement he held. Consequently, he retired to Chenjiagou where he lived out the rest of his days. It is not hard to imagine the frustration that this warrior, pensioned off at the peak of his powers, must have felt. It was during this period that he began to compile a unique form of martial art combining various disciplines and assimilating the essence of many martial skills existing at the time.

In developing his new art, Chen Wangting appears to have been heavily influenced by the famous general and outstanding military strategist Qi Jiguang (1528–1587). Qi was most famous for defending China against rampaging pirates from Japan. He also defeated Mongolian invaders from the north. His tactics involved feigning weakness and retreating before the enemy. After leading them far inland and lulling them into a false sense of superiority, Qi's forces overwhelmed

4

the invaders in a sudden and decisive counterattack (Millinger & Fang, 1976: 220–224). Chen Wangting adopted this as taijiquan's central tenet of "not meeting strength with strength" and "leading an opponent into emptiness."

General Qi Jiguang – the general
whose book on military strategy provided
inspiration for the new art of taijiquan.

Between 1559 and 1561, General Qi compiled his classic text on strategy and martial arts, *New Book of Effective Techniques* (*Ji Qiao Xinshu*). This comprehensive manual is comprised of fourteen chapters with four dedicated to the practice of *gongfu/wushu*. The most widely quoted chapter is the "Boxing Canon" (*Quan Jing*), which depicts an effective and powerful repertoire assimilating the arts of sixteen different martial systems of the time (Gaffney & Sim, 2002: 15). Like Chen Wangting later, Qi placed great emphasis on martial effectiveness, deriding the use of "flowery fists and embroidered legs" (movements that are spectacular to look at, but of no practical use).

"Chen Wangting and Qi Jiguang were not of the same dynasty, but Chen admired Qi's patriotism and the way he had absorbed the best of the various martial schools. He was especially influenced by Qi's arrangement of the different martial systems. Society was in turmoil during the period of Chen Wangting's middle age and the country was being invaded by foreigners. Unable to do his duty for the country and unable to fulfill his ambitions, Chen Wangting retired to the village with his constant companion, the *Huangting Jing* (*The Yellow Chamber's Internal and External Canon*) with the intention of organizing the different martial arts systems of his time. In this way Chen Wangting, following Qi Jiguang, is renowned for the research and collation of folk martial arts. This was the base from where he later created taijiquan" (Chen, 2004: 3).

Chen, however, did more than simply incorporate the essential theories of Qi Jiguang. His new system was highly innovative adding the novel concepts of hiding firmness in softness and using different movements to overcome the opponent's unpredictable and changing moves, thereby raising external fighting skills to a higher level. Power is generated from within, with the use of "internal energy to become outward strength." This theory is embodied in Chen's *Song of the Boxing Canon*: "Actions are varied and executed in a way that is completely unpredictable to the opponent, and I rely on twining movements and numerous hand-touching actions. 'Hand-touching' denotes the close contact of the arms to develop sensitivity to react quickly—nobody knows me, while I alone know everybody'" (Chen, 2004: 3).

In a poem written not long before his death, Chen Wangting reflected: "Sighing for past years when I was strong and sharp. Sweeping away dangerous obstacles without fear! All the favors bestowed on me by the emperor are in vain. Now old and fragile, I am left only with the book of Huang Ting for company. In moments of listlessness I study martial arts. In times of activity I cultivate the land. In leisure I teach disciples and descendants so that they may be worthy members of society" (Gaffney & Sim, 2002: 12–13).

Chen Changxing — Breaking with Tradition

Up until the time of Chen Changxing (1771–1853), the fourteenth generation of the Chen clan, taijiquan was a closely guarded family secret. Chen Changxing carried out escort duties to neighboring bandit lands, particularly in Shandong Province. His words revealed a no-nonsense approach to combat that balanced the physical and psychological aspects necessary to be successful. For example, in his *Important Words on Martial Applications*, Chen Changxing wrote: "To get the upper hand in fighting, look around and examine the shape of the ground. Hands must be fast, feet light. Examine the opponent's movements like a cat. Heart (mind) must be in order and clear.... If the hands arrive and the body also arrives [at the same moment], then defeating the enemy is like smashing a weed" (Chen X., 1990: 226).

Chen Changxing –
the first person to teach taijiquan
to someone outside the Chen clan.

Chen Changxing seems to have been a practical individual not afraid to break with tradition. The original art passed down from Chen Wangting's time had five boxing routines that Chen Changxing synthesized into what is known today as the old frame first routine (*laojia yilu*) and second routine (*laojia erlu*), also known as the Cannon Fist form (*paochui*). These make up the foundation forms from which subsequent generations of Chen Village practitioners have developed their capabilities (Chen X., 2003). The change from the original forms represents the biggest change of all in the evolution of Chen taijiquan.

Chen Changxing's second momentous break with tradition was to teach taijiquan to Yang Luchan (1799–1871)—the first time the art had been transmitted to someone outside the Chen clan. While today this may not sound so startling, at the time, the significance of the clan cannot be over-emphasized. In fact, the secrecy of the rural family clans is an important reason why many family martial systems were able to develop their own unique characteristics and flavor. A vital condition for the development of the many local fighting systems was the patriarchal family system. The primary importance traditionally placed on the family, it's setting itself strictly apart from other clans, and its autonomous way of life preserved the distinctive family combat systems over generations (but also often led to the gradual stagnation and eventual disappearance of many family systems). Outsiders were strictly excluded from learning clan secrets. By breaking this taboo, Chen paved the way for the development of the widely practiced Yang style taijiquan and thereon to other taiji styles.

Doorway leading to the
courtyard where Chen Changxing
taught Yang Luchan, creator
of Yang style taijiquan.

Today, when most people practice martial arts for sport, health, and recreation, it is easy to lose sight of the life and death seriousness of martial skill in the past. A *Shaolin Yu Taiji* magazine article refers to Wu Wenhan's book *The Complete Book of the Essence and Applications of Wu [Yuxiang] Style Taijiquan* that contains a fascinating insight into Chen taijiquan's combat history. It relates two official government documents that record the defense of Huaiqing County (where Chenjiagou is located) against the Taiping Rebellion army in 1853. One is entitled "Veritable Record of Taiping Army Attacking Huaiqing County," written by Tian Guilin, who was responsible for "defending the western town" in Huaiqing. The other is the "Daily Records of Huaiqing Defense," compiled by local school teacher Ye Zhiji (Jian, G., 2002).

Neither Tian nor Ye were taijiquan practitioners. Both were government officials, and hence their accounts can be considered somewhat objective descriptions of the events. According to the documents, once the Taiping army crossed the Yellow River and attacked Huaiqing County, the local militia was defeated and dispersed, and government troops escaped. Of all the villages, only Chenjiagou resisted. In his "Veritable Record Under the 29th Day of the 5th Month," Tian notes:

> The head of the thieves (i.e. Taiping rebels) called Big Headed Ram (*Datou Yang*) invaded Chenjiagou. This thief was extremely bold and strong; he was able to carry two big canons under his arms and swiftly attack the town. The battles that destroyed whole towns were conducted under the command of this thief. Fortunately, Chen Zhongshen and Chen Jishen, two brothers from Chenjiagou, were very skilled in using spears and long poles. They used long poles to pull Big Headed Ram down from the horse, and then they cut his head off. The thieves got very angry, and the whole group went on to Zhaobao Jie burning everything, then to Henei and villages around Baofeng, and no soldiers came to their rescue [of these areas, fortunately Chen Zhongshen and others managed to escape]. – Jian, G., 2002

The documents stated that only the inhabitants of Chenjiagou took an active part in the resistance against the Taiping rebels. This would imply that, unlike the other villages in the area, Chenjiagou had a stronger martial tradition and used it to defend itself (Jian G., 2002).

The Modern Era

During the early years of the 20th century, taijiquan practice in Chenjiagou reached its zenith, with almost everyone in the village training in the art. At the same time, the establishment of a taijiquan school and a more formalized teaching syllabus led to the development of many famous practitioners. To express their respect for the family art, the villagers reconstructed many of the dwellings of famous practitioners of the past and built many taijiquan related structures (Wang, J., 2006: 4).

However, the good times were not to last and the fall of the Qing Dynasty in 1912 brought a resurgence of regional warlordism to many parts of China, including Henan Province (Hucker, 1975: 328). On top of this, much of China suffered a period of devastating natural disasters. During the early 1920's, much of Henan Province, along with the neighboring provinces of Shandong, Shanxi, Shaanxi, and Hebei, suffered a catastrophic period of famine caused by the severe droughts of 1919. In *The Search for Modern China*, Jonathan Spence described a shattered scene: "In farm villages … the combination of withered crops and inadequate government relief was disastrous: at least 500,000 people died, and out of an estimated 48.8 million in these five provinces, over 19.8 million were declared destitute" (Spence, 1999: 298–299). Villagers were reduced to eating straw and leaves and epidemics such as typhus cut a swathe through many too frail to fight back.

The disastrous combination of events meant that the numbers of people practicing taijiquan in the village was getting less and less as people left the village to escape the hardships. In 1928, Chen Fake (1887–1957), a 17th-generation Chen clan master, went to Beijing to teach at the request of his nephew, Chen Zhaopei. In those days, travel was difficult and Beijing must have seemed like the other side of the world to villagers most of whom had spent their entire lives in the village. One can imagine the somber mood the night before he was to leave when Chen Fake went to the family temple to bid farewell to his fellow villagers and demonstrate his taijiquan one last time. Chen Liqing, a noted small frame (*xiaojia*) practitioner was a young child at the time, and witnessed the event. She recalled, "Chen Fake demonstrated laojia yilu. During the emitting power (*fajing*) movements, you could hear the power from the wind created that made the candle-flames flicker. At that time, the temple was made of mud and, when he stamped his foot, five of the roof tiles were dislodged and came down. One person tried to test his strength and was bounced off the wall. When he finished, he saluted those present in the room" (Chen, L., 2005).

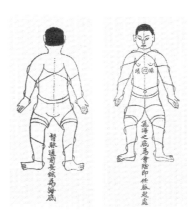

Chen taijiquan's silk reeling energy depicted in Chen Xin's
Illustrated Explanation of Chen Taijiquan.

Chen Zhaopei, who had left the village shortly before Chen Fake to teach taijiquan throughout China, was deeply troubled that there was no one left in the village to transmit taijiquan to the next generation. He had learned taijiquan from several renowned masters, including his uncles Chen Fadou and Chen Fake, and village elders Chen Yanxi and Chen Xin. In 1958, after retiring, the 65-year old Zhaopei assumed the daunting responsibility himself, returning home to Chenjiagou to revive the practice of taijiquan.

Chen Zhaopei – the teacher who revived taijiquan practice in Chenjiagou.

Chen Zhaopei's son, Chen Kesen recalled his father's decision to pick up the mantle of preserving taijiquan in its birthplace: "He willingly returned to the spartan village life of Chenjiagou. After he returned to the village, he set up a taijiquan school in his own home, bearing all of the costs himself. At the same time, he also set up a training class in the county town, Wenxian, teaching members of the government, the workers and staff of the Mining School, as well as coaching the teachers and students. There was a vigorous renaissance of taijiquan in old Wenxian. Who knew that this good scene would not last for long" (Chen, 1993)?

Chen Zhaopei set about improving and tightening the standards of Chen taijiquan in the village, bringing under his tutelage many new devotees. The resurrection of the dwindling Chen family taijiquan is generally attributed to this period. His most celebrated disciples today are Chen Xiaowang, Wang Xi'an, Zhu Tiancai, and Chen Zhenglei, described collectively as the "Four Buddha's Warriors" by a journalist in the early 1980's. All were sent out to take part in various competitions and demonstrations, slowly increasing Chen taijiquan's profile (Zhu, 2000). The combination of his affectionate and easy-going nature and serious attitude to training attracted many students. Reminiscing about this period, Chen Xiaowang remembered: "at that time, learning from my uncle Chen Zhaopei was very grueling" (Chen, X., 2005: 76).

An early picture of Chen Xiaowang –
19th generation standard bearer.

The Impact of the Cultural Revolution

In 1966, Mao Zedong and his close supporters instigated the Cultural Revolution, an immense and distorted movement that for ten years inflicted fear and anarchy on China. By arousing peasant-powered mass violence, Mao let loose a whirlwind of social turmoil. Individuals deemed to be a "four bad-categories element" (*silei fenzi*) were labeled as "bad class" and suffered severe discrimination. The four groups were defined as: landlord, rich peasant, counterrevolutionary, and rotten element. Throughout the countryside, anyone unlucky enough to be branded within these categories was shown little mercy in the highly emotional environment during the "Maoist struggle sessions." In *The Class System in Rural China: A Case Study*, Jonathan Unger documented the creation of caste-like pariah groups and their maltreatment during the post-revolutionary period. His study focused upon a small rural community in Guangdong Province (coincidentally also called Chen Village) with many similarities to Chenjiagou: "As a symbol of polluted status, during the 1960s and 1970s the dozen or so elderly 'four bad elements' … had to sweep dung from the village square before mass meetings were held there. To symbolize further that most of them were irredeemably among the damned, they were not permitted to attend any political sessions or participate in Mao study groups" (Unger, 1984: 121–141).

At its heart, the Cultural Revolution demanded a comprehensive assault on the "four old" elements within Chinese society: "old customs, old habits, old culture, and old thinking" (Spence, 1999: 575). During this period, the Red Guard burned many historic taijiquan documents. One story recounts how Wang Xi'an was deeply upset to see the destruction of such irreplaceable manuscripts. Coming

11

into possession of one such document, Wang wrapped it in plastic and plastered it into the ceiling of his home. Discovery of his actions could have had dire consequences both to himself and his family.

Copy of a painting of Chen Wangting
lost during the Cultural Revolution.

During the Cultural Revolution and the period of civil unrest just preceding it, most taijiquan related structures in the village were destroyed (Wang, J., 2006: 6). The location of Chen Changxing's grave was lost with the removal of its headstone and a number of priceless artifacts were lost, including Chen Wangting's sword and a portrait of Chen Wangting with Jiang Fa. Disastrously for taijiquan's progress, many taiji experts suffered greatly throughout this time.

Right:
Chen Xiaoxing –
Principal of Chenjiagou
Taijiquan School.

Below:
Training in the Chenjiagou
Taijiquan School courtyard.

The combination of incessant Maoist indoctrination with hard labor was the norm in villages all over China throughout the Cultural Revolution. Chen Xiaoxing, the principal of the Chenjiagou Taijiquan School, recalled how he was required to work twelve hours a day in a brick factory (Chen, X., 2003). Chen Kesen recalled how his father, Chen Zhaopei, was persecuted and subjected to humiliating public "struggle sessions" during the Cultural Revolution, but coura-geously taught secretly at night. The courage of his prized disciples led him to compose the following verse: "At eighty years I teach taiji, without concern for whether the road ahead is bad or good. The wind howls, the rain beats down, and the difficulties are many. I delight in seeing the next generation of successors fill-ing my home village" (Chen K., 1993).

In a radio interview conducted in the United Kingdom for BBC Radio's "Eastern Horizon," Chen Zhenglei (one of the four Buddha's Warriors) explained: "The biggest setback for taijiquan and all martial arts was during the Cultural Revolution when people were not able to practice freely and martial arts became outlawed. Taijiquan and other martial arts diminished in China. When China opened its gates again to the rest of the world, its rich culture was promoted and martial arts became standardized and simplified in the process. This had its pros and cons—it allows more people to learn, but this ultimately dilutes and changes the virtues of the traditional form" (Feng, 2004: 33–34).

Training the posture Buddha's
Warrior Attendant Pounds Mortar.
Chen Xiaoxing at front.

The author pushing hands
with Chen Xiaoxing.

However, from the mid-1970's, the political climate began to soften and the outlook became brighter for taijiquan in Chenjiagou. In 1974, the eighteenth-generation standard-bearer, Chen Zhaokui, son of Chen Fake, returned to the village to teach the new frame (*xinjia*). In 1978, a host of new writings was given wide circulation through the state-controlled press. "Focusing on the horrors and tragedies experienced by many in the Cultural Revolution, this 'literature of the wounded,' as it was called, stimulated debate and reflection about China's past and its future prospects. Signs seemed to point to a cultural thaw, among which one could include the convening of a conference (in far-off Kunming in Yunnan admittedly) to study the long-taboo subject of comparative religion, with papers delivered on Buddhism and Daoism, Islam and Christianity" (Spence, 1999: 621).

Opening Up of China

Chen-style taijiquan has enjoyed a surge of popularity around the world in the last few decades. As the current generation of masters from Chenjiagou finally got the opportunity to travel and demonstrate their skills, more and more people have been exposed to the traditional village art. Before, to many, taijiquan was synonymous with the more widely seen Yang style with its characteristic slow movements and even tempo, or the various government approved versions of taiji e.g. Simplified 24-Step, etc.

Since the change of national policy and the opening up of China's economy, the district government has begun the process of building up Chenjiagou again. As the birthplace of taijiquan, the village carries with it profound cultural and historical significance of interest not just in China, but to the world over. Plans are afoot to develop Chenjiagou as a tourist attraction. In recent years, the district government has invited architects from Beijing to survey and plan projects. At present, nothing definite has been decided and the only officially designated tourist attractions in the village are the Taiji Temple and the house where Yang Luchan learned taijiquan (Chen, B., 2005).

Twentieth-generation practitioner Chen Bing optimistically looks forward to the day when Chenjiagou and taijiquan will go out into the international arena on a scale to match the nearby Shaolin Temple. However, he notes the caveat of the need for higher-level government support: "If the central government takes an interest, then the steps toward development will be much lighter. Individual influence is small and if you just rely on the villagers, teachers, and instructors, the development will be much slower and smaller. You need the infrastructure behind it and at the moment the climate is favorable" (Chen, B., 2005).

References

Chen, B. (2005, Sep 12). Personal interview conducted in Chenjiagou by members of Chenjiagou Taijiquan GB (Great Britain).

Chen, K. (1993 Apr 22). My father, Chen Zhaopei, *Henan Sports Journal*. Downloaded from website: www.chenstyle.com.

Chen, L. (2005). Interview downloaded from website: www.chenjiagou.net.

Chen, X. (2003 Dec 5). Personal interview conducted in Chenjiagou by members of Chenjiagou Taijiquan GB (Great Britain).

Chen, X. (2005). China's living treasure. *Chinatown – the Magazine*, No. 18: 75–77.

Chen, X. (2004). *Chen family taijiquan of China*. Zhengzhou, Henan, China: Henan People's Publishing.

Chen, X. (1990). *Chen Style Taijiquan transmitted through generations*. Beijing, China: People's Sports Publishing.

Chen, Z. (n.d.). *Eastern Horizon*, BBC Radio program interview.

Feng, N. (2004). Chen Zhenglei. *Chinatown – the Magazine*, No. 8: 33–34.

Gaffney, D. & Sim, D. (2002). *Chen Style Taijiquan: The source of taiji boxing*. Berkeley, CA: North Atlantic Books.

Hiebert, P., Shaw, R., & Tienou, T. (1999). *Understanding folk religion*. Grand Rapids, MI: Baker Books.

Hucker, C. (1975). *China's imperial past: An introduction to Chinese history and culture*. Stanford, CA: Stanford University Press.

Jian, G. (2002). The small frame of Chen style taijiquan. *Shaolin Yu Taiji*, 9. Downloaded from website: www.taiji-bg.com.

Millinger, J. & Fang C. (1976). Ch'i Chi-kuang, in *Dictionary of Ming biography, 1368–1644*. Goodrich, L. & Fang, C. (Eds.). New York City, NY: Columbia University Press.

Spence, J. (1999). *The search for modern China*. New York City, NY: Norton.

Unger, J. (1984). *The class system in rural China: A case study in class and social stratification in post-revolution China*. Watson, J. (Ed.). Cambridge, UK: Cambridge University Press.

Wang, J., et al. (2006). *Chenjiagou research*. Zhengzhou, Henan, China: Henan Agricultural University Research Centre.

Zhu, T. (2000, Aug. 17). Personal interview conducted in Singapore by members of Chenjiagou Taijiquan GB (Great Britain).

Comments on Selections from Chen Xin's *Illustrated Explanations* of *Chen Taijiquan* with Commentary from Chen Xiaowang

by Stephan Berwick, M.A., &
translations by Dannie Butler, M.A.

Leading representative of the Chen Family system
of taijiquan, Grandmaster Chen Xiaowang
demonstrates a few classic postures.
All photos courtesy of Chen Xiaowang.

Introduction

Historically, the level of boxing skill in Chenjiagou—the Chen family village from where taijiquan originated—always matched the times. During war and crises, skill levels dipped as compared to the high levels of skill exhibited during times of peace and prosperity. The 16th generation Chen family scholar, Chen Xin (1849–1929, also known as Chen Pinsan) divided his time between boxing practice and scholarly pursuits. When Chen Xin's highly influential classic, *Illustrated Explanations of Chen Taijiquan,* was published in 1933, the level of taiji in Chenjiagou was considered good, according to Chen Xiaowang. Chen Xin was a distant relative of today's acknowledged standard bearer of the 19th generation, Chen Xiaowang.

Regardless of the fluctuating quality in actual practice, taijiquan has always been subject to theoretical debate. The absence of any definitive publications emanating from Chenjiagou contributed to this, since Chen taijiquan theory was never recorded until the publication of Chen Xin's work. Hand written in classical Chinese and published posthumously, it took Chen Xin over twelve years to write the book, from the 34th year of emperor Guangxu's reign (1908) until the 8th year after the formation of China's first republican government (1919). He produced four volumes containing hundreds of distinct classical Chinese characters. Of note, the well-known Chen taiji concept of silk-reeling energy (*chansijing*) is a central theme throughout the book. Chen Xin successfully meshed the profound principles of the *Yijing* (*Book of Changes*), yin/yang theory, meridian theory, and practical technical descriptions, to produce a boxing manual of unprecedented comprehensiveness (Wu & Wu, 1976: 19).

The technical details of core Chen taiji technique contained in this seminal work have never been fully conveyed by and for contemporary practitioners. One must be able to read classical Chinese (a rarity even among most fluent Chinese readers) and have an intimate understanding of taiji to assimilate the book's contents. Thus combining the language skills and taiji experience of the authors, this chapter provides the first-ever detailed English translations and analysis of some of the most complex technical sections from Chen Xin's work—along with commentary from Chen Xiaowang.

While Chen Xin's publication remains a masterwork on taijiquan, "the book itself is not enough to understand taiji," according to Chen Xiaowang. "Just language is not enough," he asserts. He insists that "Nobody, in any language, can write about taiji with true clarity and accuracy." He maintains that "hands-on corrections are more effective than any book."

Readers familiar with Chen family teaching methods, know that success in the art is largely based on a foundation of strict body structural skills that build the unique internal power (*jing*) characteristic of Chen taiji. Based on his insistence that skill development is based on "feeling," Chen Xiaowang has developed accessible teaching methods to instill the "feeling" of appropriate body structure, as Chen Xin sought to explain in his masterwork.

Chen Xiaowang teaches that "three languages are necessary to understand taiji":

The language of speaking and writing: To explain and theorize
The language of the body: To demonstrate and see
The language of corrections: To feel (the most important language)

The principles described by Chen Xin and as taught today by masters such as Chen Xiaowang apply to all versions of Chen taiji. Chen Xiaowang maintains that the principles described by Chen Xin permeate every variation of Chen taijiquan.

One of the principles expressed by Chen Xin in a particular chapter of his writings is a well-defined sense of purpose for practicing martial arts. While small portions of this chapter, "Essential Knowledge for the Study of Taijiquan," have been translated, the whole essay has not received a full translation and/or analysis of the context from which it was written. To that end, the authors include this essay in its entirety, with commentary, to enlighten and inspire readers' martial practice.

As an aid for readers, photos of Chen Xiaowang in the postures chosen for this article are presented along with Chen Xin's original hand drawn images. Also, Chen Xiaowang and Mr. Berwick's analysis is in regular type placed above the translated text which is emphasized by a gray line running parallel to the text, with a few comments in brackets from Mr. Butler and Mr. Berwick appearing throughout where applicable.

To help readers follow Chen Xin's diagrams and his highly detailed descriptions, he wrote:

> When doing taijiquan, it is not usually necessary to adhere to a specific direction. However, there is a certain standard for the pictures. The Big Dipper leads the heavens in the north, so it is appropriate that north is the primary direction. Therefore, in order to specify directions, the drawings all face north, with right corresponding to the east, left to the west, and the rear to the south.

The most influential technique of Chen taiji, Single Whip permeates all later forms of taiji and holds profound meaning for both internal development and combat usage. Single Whip's practical applications depend on a sophisticated use of body skills and can be considered an "internal" interpretation of similar boxing techniques commonly seen in ancient Northern Chinese boxing forms. Chen taiji's silk-reeling energy (*chansijing*) is highly refined when practicing Single Whip correctly. Thus, Chen Xin included supplementary diagrams to illustrate the silk-reeling pathways that imbue Single Whip.

Chen Xiaowang expresses the principles described by Chen Xin as, "In the beginning, the outside (external) moves the inside (internal). When one's *qi* achieves a state of 60% qi "flowing," this feeling or sense of qi flow becomes more tangible and can then be controlled by the mind." And as described throughout Chen Xin's requirements for Single Whip, Chen Xiaowang's famed grandfather, Chen Fake, defined the internal energy of the crown of the head "as the essential qi from the heart" (Kohler, 1991: 14).

SINGLE WHIP

The central *qi* [or intrinsic energy] at the top of the head is the true qi. The intention of the mind leads it upward and it rises to the top of the head. The central qi is led up naturally; no object moves it. Thus is the intention.

When doing taijiquan, the mind is the ruler. The spine is key in moving the body left or right. The waist is key in moving the body up and down. The waist is raised by raising the qi. The waist is lowered by lowering the qi. Although it seems that there is a contention between raising and lowering, there is actually one qi throughout and raising and lowering are not at odds with each other. The left foot is led by the left hand. The right foot is led by the right hand. As for how the hands move at the top, and how the lower body and feet move at the bottom, everything rises and falls together. Top and bottom follow each other and naturally move in unison.

Moving the hands lies entirely in the palms and fingers leading the movements of the entire body. It is particularly important that the feet follow the hands. The central qi must move slowly through the forearms and upper arms. One must not become flustered and neglect to follow the natural principle. Moving naturally, do not favor one side. By means of the mind, the qi moves through both forearms. This is central qi. The back of the left hand faces north 10 to 20 percent. The back of the right hand faces the left hand 40 to 50 percent. The center qi moves to the fingers. This completely fulfills closure of the whole.

A: Force is used in the center of the fingers.

B: The left wrist must not be limp.

C: The inside of the elbow resembles the new moon or a bow, which is slightly bent.

D: The eyes focus on the middle finger of the left hand.

E: The energy of the top of the head leads upward. The top of the head is straight up.

G: The front and rear shoulders both collapse and must not rise up.

H: The right wrist must not be limp. The fingers of the right hand all pinch together at one point. The front hand extends. The fingers of the rear hand restrain. This is the rear hand.

I: The front and edge of the palm use force. The back of the palm and the thumb use force.

J: Chest.

K: This space resembles the shape of the new moon.

L: The horizontal qi in the diaphragm is moved to the bottom of the feet. If one cannot do this, one should still move it to the *dantian* [lower abdomen].

M: The front knee bears the weight horizontally. The front knee sticks out fifty or sixty percent.

N: The toes of the left foot must grip the ground with force. The big toe especially must use force.

O: The left foot is slightly emptier than the right foot.

P: The heel first touches the ground, then the foot gradually comes forward until the left toes touch the ground.

Q: The groin is empty and round. Everything closes toward the center and naturally correlates.

R: The right knee sticks out twenty or thirty percent. It must not be limp, but must bear weight.

S: The right foot faces north. It hooks slightly to the northwest.

T: There is a hollow in the *yong quan*.[1]

U: The heel must press on the ground with force. Only then will there be stability.

V: The right foot must be full. This is called "the front empty, the rear full."

W: The two thighs embrace inward from the outside.

X: The pelvis turns slightly upward and the lower abdomen closes. The groin is then rounded. A pulsing naturally occurs.

Y: The left hand? It closes with the right.

Z: The right hand should close with the left.

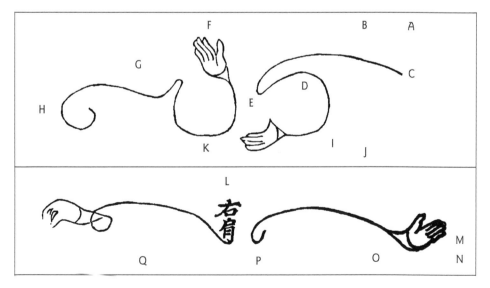

Hand Silk-Reeling in Single Whip

A: This diagram goes with the diagram above. It faces north, and focuses on the right hand.

B: This is the closing of left and right. It is the transitional pulse between the previous posture and the next posture.

C: The left fingers are open and together. The forearm is relaxed. The left hand makes a circle and then moves west from below. The forearm is relaxed.

D: Starting point for the left hand.

E: Waist.

F: Hand starts.

G: The right hand moves thus.

H: The right hand stops.

I: The left hand leaves the waist and moves upward.

J: Before moving, the hand first makes a small circle and closes with the right.

K: This is *ge bo jin* [arm energy]. When the hand has turned enough, the back of the hand will be slightly forward.

L: Left shoulder.

M: The left hand stops. The left hand opens (unfolds).

N: Because this diagram also faces north, left and right are as above.

O: This is a diagram of the movement of the left hand. The left forearm bends to close with the right forearm.

P: The left hand begins. In the center, in the chest and abdomen, qi is exchanged from the *tiantu* acupoint to the lower abdomen. The *qi hai, shi men,* and *guan yuan* are like a *qing* [chime stone, made by hollowing out a hard sonorous stone], curved like a bow.[2] This is known as "hollowing the chest." It is closed. The energy must be insubstantial.

Q: The right forearm is turned backward and closes with the left hand.

R: The line in the circle is where the right hand originates. Before it originates, the right hand makes a small circle. The right hand restrains.

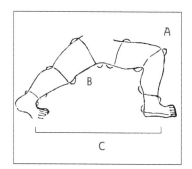

Lower Body Silk-Reeling in Single Whip

The reeling is from the foot to the base formed at the top of the thighs. The energy reels from outside to inside. When it reels from the base and spirals back in the legs, hard qi is not used in the energy of the legs. When the knee closes inward, the five toes all close inward. The leg naturally closes from top to bottom, and the groin is naturally rounded.

Method for Moving the Feet

The left foot first comes beside the right foot, with the toes touching the ground. It then steps out toward the west. The two feet are approximately one and a half feet apart.

A: Left knee
B: Right knee
C: Diagram of correspondence between left and right energy

Method for Moving the Rear Heel

It need not be mentioned again that in Single Whip the left foot is first beside the right foot with the toes touching the ground, and then steps toward the west. As for the right foot, in the Lazily Tying Coat [lan ca yi] posture, the toes are pointing toward the northeast. When the left foot takes a step to the left, the toes face northwest. Just prior to the left toes touching the ground, the right foot remains on the ground and the toes are facing northeast. The right heel twists on the ground toward the northwest, that is toward the west but slightly north. Therefore, it is said that the right toes and left toes touch the ground at the same time. The left foot touches the ground heel first then gradually comes down until the toes touch the ground. The left foot and right foot are closed. Only thus is the energy (jin) not dissipated.

If one asks what is meant by "Single Whip," the answer would be that the two arms are not in front of the chest, but out to left and right sides of the body. When the left and right forearms extend, the motion seems weak, but it is actually as dangerous as a whip. The extension of the two forearms also resembles a whip. From this the posture gets its name. The left hand is primary. It moves upward until it is level with the navel, then makes a small circle from outside to inside. The right hand makes a small circle forward from the rear. The right and left close. As for the spirit, it should be as though two people were facing each other and talking.

After this, from the closed position, the left hand leads the left side of the body from bottom to top toward the west. It then moves gradually toward the west, stopping at about 80 or 90 percent. While the left hand is extending, the eyes follow the left hand, and when the hand stops, the eyes remain focused on the middle finger of the left hand and do not look elsewhere.

As for the central qi, the reeling method is the same as that for the right hand and right forearm in the lazily tying coat posture. When closing, the left foot is first pulled in beside the right foot with the toes touching the ground. This creates a posture for the next movement of the feet. When moving, the left foot moves toward the west together with the left hand. The left heel touches the ground as the left hand is about to stop. Movement continues until the left big toe touches the ground and the left hand stops at the same time. The form appears to stop, but the spirit does not stop. The left side of the body from top to bottom follows the extension of the left foot, which varies with the size of the person but is no less than approximately two feet.

As for the right hand, when closing it first makes a circle. When the left hand rises and moves toward the west, the right wrist is back. The right hand moves forward and then makes another circle. The arm slowly twists counter-clockwise. This differs from the opening of the left hand. Not only is there energy in the right arm as it twists, but it also moves slightly toward the east and the back of the hand closes toward the front. Since the right hand moves toward the east while the left hand moves toward the west, it appears that there are two separate motions. Actually, they are the same in spirit. The reason the back of the right hand twists forward is to lower the pulse for the next move.

As for why the right fingers close together and remain closed, this is to prevent someone from grabbing the fingers from behind and bending them back, since the eyes are focused forward.

The silk-reeling energy in the right arm spirals from the shoulder to the forearm, then to the right fingers. Although the right foot does not move, it twists based on the movement of the right hand. At first the toes are toward the northeast. Then as the right hand moves, the right heel remains on the ground while the toes twist toward the northwest. The right side of the body from top to bottom moves in this motion.

When the method is explained, it must necessarily be divided into parts. However, one must not take this to mean that it is actually divided. What is meant by "closed" is that the entire body closes together. Only then is there excellence.

As for the joints of the body, such as the left and right elbows and left and right shoulders, corresponding left and right joints must close and face each other. This needs no further explanation.

Those who do not understand may look at the illustration and copy the method once they have comprehended it. Everything goes back to keeping straight. One must not lean to one side. The joints must be relaxed, and the arms must simply hang from the shoulders. The movements seem soft, but they are actually hard. The spirit is hidden within rather than revealed. This is great skill.

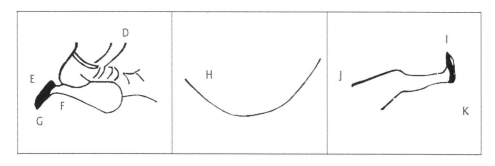

OVERHEAD CANNON

25

The Overhead Cannon features Chen taiji's unique torque-like expression of explosive power releases (*fajing*). Usually seen at the end of the first form (*yilu*), this technique contains applications from striking to lesser known throwing techniques. Chen Xin's description of Overhead Cannon's "pounding attack" (described below) does not just refer to pounding with the fists. He is likely referring to the defender using his body to pound the opponent at close range, from the side. Also, considering that Chen taiji can be considered a grappling art, his attentive descriptions of how the feet grip the ground, along with how the bodily joints "close" are similar to wrestling concepts taught globally.

The name of this posture describes its main movement, which is combined with a placement of the feet to form the posture. "Overhead Cannon" refers to using a pounding attack against someone in front.

The left and right hands descend and move from the front to the right and back. From the right and back they rotate forward making a large circle, then seizing and pounding downward in front of the chest. The left hand [although the term "hand" is used, the forearm is also included] uses rotational energy and the right hand uses counter-rotational energy. The left leg uses rotational energy and the right leg uses counter-rotational energy. The feet are placed as has been described. The right and left elbows face outward. The right and left pound with the arms and fingers facing upward. From top to bottom, the four limbs all use embracing energy. This is the energy in the center of the chest. It descends from the upper left, then rises and makes a circle from right to left. The chest closes toward the front. Groin energy is open, rounded, and closed. The toes of both feet face inward and the energy is closed. Top of the head energy leads. The two shoulders, two knees, and two heels all turn in from the outside. The combined strength is concentrated in the pounding motion. The eyes look between the two hands. This move is called "Protecting the Heart" pounding motion. It is very similar to the first move, Jin Gang Works the Pestle. In both moves, Protecting the Heart is paramount. If the heart is not shaken, the top, bottom, and all four sides can be handled without error.

Explanation of the Joints

All joints in the entire body face each other and the energy is closed. The qi is one from top to bottom and the energy is closed.

A: The energy of the waist descends. If it does not, there will be no strength at the bottom of the foot, and the groin cannot be closed.
B: The two elbows face outward, and the two fists face each other, one forward, one back. The energy is closed.
C: The two shoulders are relaxed and lowered. Do not raise them.
D: The energy of the top of the head leads. Downward extension of this energy is the key to a strong body.
E: The eyes focus on the left elbow and left fist.
F: The chest must face forward and be closed. It must be entirely empty. The countless forms all contain extreme emptiness.
G: The right foot hooks toward the inside. The inside of the heel kicks back. The toes close inward.
H: The right knee is slightly bent. With the knee bent, the groin opens.
I: The groin must be large. It must be empty. It must be round. It must be closed.

J: The big toe closes to the inside. The five toes and the heel all use force to grip the ground. The left knee is bent. Do not extend it beyond the toe.

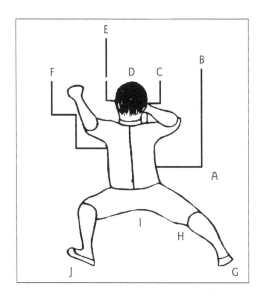

FALLING SPLIT
Grandmaster Chen Xiaowang in a
variation of Falling Split. The posture
is low, but not touching the ground.

27

This is a signature movement from Chen taiji's first form (*yilu*), and Chen Xin's explication of this technique holds noteworthy historical details. It is the earliest written record documenting how this technique was practiced before the recent incarnations of this maneuver. All major schools of Chen taiji today practice this seminal movement in a sliding manner, usually with a stomp of the right foot to propel the left leg into a half split. In Chen taiji's early history, the Falling Split (or "Dragon Creeps Down") was practiced with a high vertical leap, falling into the half split position.

Leaping into leg splitting postures is common in many traditional Northern Chinese boxing systems. According to the commonly accepted history of Chen Taiji, Yang Luchan's teacher, Chen Changxing (of whom Chen Xiaowang is a direct descendant), is largely credited with removing the leaping motion when he standardized the original Chen family forms into the two highly dense, well-honed open-hand routines that survive to this day.

Of particular note, Chen Xin describes the seldom understood fighting application of Falling Split. His clear description of this movement's usage reveals that this classic Chen taiji maneuver boasts a simple combat utility that demands both high athletic and internal skills.

What is meant by Falling Split is that the body falls from the air and the legs form a split. The diagram shows the left leg extended out and the right leg bent. This is a single split. With a double split, it is impossible to rise again without a leap. This differs from the single split, in which the left heel is extended foward and closed and the right knee is outward and open. One can fall or rise by turning the right heel with force. This is slightly easier, and most practitioners use this method nowadays.

The left hand extends out with the left leg as the right leg goes down so that it gradually goes forward. The right ear listens to the right side. The right arm extends and the right hand looks as if it wants to move forward.

A: The eyes look at the left hand and left foot.
B: The top of the head energy must not be lost.
C: The left leg extends out and falls flat on the ground. The left foot kicks the enemy's shin. The left knee must not bend. The body must draw the qi and collapse forward. The right knee bends, but must not rest fully on the ground. The hip bone is almost in a sitting posture, and there is an element of emptiness in its fullness. The top of the right foot faces down and the bottom of the shoe faces up. The Falling Split is reminiscent of the double rise. Whereas in the double rise one flies upward into the air, here one falls from mid-air and the two legs land on the ground. It is a natural correspondence rather than an artificial one. This adheres strictly to ancient precepts on devising routines. When the legs have been placed, the right arm is bent and the left arm is extended. Both hands are to the left. Both hands then circle upward from the lower left to the right. The right arm unfolds and the left arm is bent. Both hands extend. At this point, the right leg falls to the ground. As the right heel nears the ground, the left leg kicks out toward the southwest. The idea is for the movement of the left foot to resemble a crescent. The left hand moves as the left leg does; from the right waist it slowly arcs downward, then pushes out to the southwest simultaneously with the left foot. At first, finger strength is used, then palm strength is used. The right arm is

28

back. Although the arm is extended, the hand still has the intention of moving downward and forward; it simply has not done so.

D: Diagram of the right leg.

E: In the Falling Split, the top of the head energy lifts, and the mind energy lifts the foot. The chest collapses to hold the energy. The hip bone is not completely seated. When the right foot comes down from mid-air, the bottom of the foot faces up.

F: The inside of the calf is empty rather than full.

G: This shows how the left foot kicks forward.

H: The left foot arcs slowly from the right and kicks forward. The heel uses force.

I: Illustration of the Left Leg Outward Kick.

J: When the left leg kicks out, the entire body's force is concentrated in the heel.

K: The main part of this move is the forward kick of the left leg. This kick is not empty. It is to kick the enemy. Therefore, the heel must use force. The forward push of the left hand is to help the left foot. The right hand is on the right side. This is also to help the left foot.

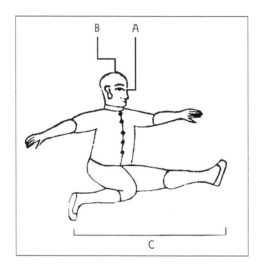

ESSENTIAL KNOWLEDGE
FOR TAIJIQUAN STUDY

One of the hallmarks of the Chen family is their long-time connection to the military. Beginning with the General Chen Wangting, credited as the founder of taijiquan, and generations later, Chen Zhongshen, who was Chen Xin's father and a documented battalion leader against rebels during the Taiping Rebellion—the Chens appear to have always been a family of warriors. Consequently, the Chen clan exhibit an unusual sense of martial pride that imbues the ethos of their boxing art with a timeless and universal sense of purpose. Of this martial spirit, Chen Xin wrote the following:

When studying taijiquan, one must be respectful. Without respect, one will be careless with his teacher or friends without, and careless with his body within When the mind has no restraint, how can one study an art?

When studying taijiquan, one must not be unruly. Unruliness will lead to trouble. One must not be unruly with his hands nor with his words. Outside, one must have the refined air of a scholar. If one is unruly outside, he will surely stray from the Mean.[3]

When studying taijiquan, one must not be complacent. Complacency will harm one's moves. As the saying goes, "Beyond the sky, there is more sky." If one can be humble, then he can accept teaching with an open mind. Who would not be willing to impart skill to him? When one's skill is the accumulated skill of many, it is great skill.

When studying taijiquan, one must carefully ponder each motion. If even a single motion is not pondered, this tendency will continue until one's reasoning is completely obscured. When something is being passed on and it is especially important to pay attention, if one does not pay attention at this point, the entire thread will become incorrect. The transitions will not be fluid, the motions will become disconnected, and it will be impossible to maintain the qi from beginning to end. If the qi cannot be maintained throughout, it will be difficult to even inquire about *tai he yuan qi* [great harmonious original qi].

When studying taijiquan, one should study books. Once the principles in books have been understood, the study of taijiquan will naturally become easier.

The study of taijiquan is the study of yin and yang, opening and closing. Yin and yang, opening and closing are already inherent in your own body. They cannot be increased or decreased through teaching. Once the inherent yin and yang, opening and closing are recovered, teaching stops. Teaching is instruction in the rule, that is, the principle of reaching perfection through the Great Mean.

Although taijiquan is not of great use, in this day many powers are contending with each other. Without martial arts, how can one survive? If this book is merely taken and practiced, it will be no small supplement to the marching drills of the army. If the people in our country practice it, then in hand-to-hand encounters with the enemy, even though the enemy may be strong, what can he do to us? This, too, then, is one way of protecting the country. Men of thought should not dismiss this as simply my humble remarks.

The study of taijiquan must not be used to rob or pillage. If one uses it to rob, then when Heaven seizes him, no supernatural spirits will help him, much less people. For who in the world can tolerate it?

The study of taijiquan must not be used to bully and oppress people. One who bullies and oppresses people incurs the wrath of everyone and is chief among evildoers.

Grandmaster
Chen Xiaowang finds
Chen Xin's theories
in taiji practice.

Notes

[1] Reference to an acupoint (K17) in the center of the bottom of the foot.

[2] Reference to acupoints located in the lower abdomen, known as the *ming men* that lies vertically along the "conception" meridian.

[3] In the introduction to the Confucian classic, the *Doctrine of the Mean*, the character *chung*, rendered "mean" here, is defined as "being without inclination to either side." The Song dynasty philosopher Chu Xi states that it is "without inclination or deflection, [and] neither exceeds nor comes short" (Legge, 1971: 382).

Bibliography

Berwick, S. (2001). Chen Xiaowang on learning, practicing, and teaching Chen taiji. *Journal of Asian Martial Arts, 10*(2), 98–101.

Berwick, S. (2001). Chen Village under the influence of Chen Xiaoxing. *Journal of Asian Martial Arts, 10*(2), 88–97.

Chen, X. (September 30, 2002). Personal interview in New York.

Chen, X. (2000). *Illustrated explanations of Chen taijiquan* (*Chen shi Taijiquan tushuo*). Shanghai: Shanghai Bookshop Publishing Company. (Original work published in 1933)

Kohler, S. (Trans.) (1991). Internal energies of Chen and Yang styles. *Tai Chi, 15*(2), 14–19. (Original work published in 1975)

Legge, J. (1971). *Confucius: Confucian analects, The great learning, & doctrine of the mean*. New York: Dover Publications. (Original work published in 1893)

Liuxin, G. & Shen, J. (Eds.) (1963). *Chen shi taijiquan*. Beijing: People's Sports Publishing Company.

Wile, D. (1999). *Tai chi ancestors: The making of an internal martial art*. New City, NY: Sweet Chi Press.

Wu, T. & Wu, T. (1976). The yin and yang of tai chi chuan. *Self Defense World, 2*(2), 18–19.

Body-Mind Connections in Chen Xin's *Illustrated Explanation of Chen-Style Taijiquan*

by Miriam O'Connor, M.A.

Chen-style Left Separate Base.
All photographs courtesy
of Michael A. DeMarco.
Photography by Pete Gool.

Introduction

The philosophy underpinning taijiquan practice is a fascinating but elusive field of study. If it is hard for researchers to record or analyze the physical dimension of a moving art, it is harder still to capture the movements of the mind and spirit that inspire these physical movements.

Since the mental world of practitioners cannot be studied directly, their writings naturally appear as the next best source of research material. Thus my own foray into this research area began with a search for a practitioner's text in classical Chinese, which I would need to translate and discuss in my thesis.[1]

Two obviously valuable texts had already been translated: *Master Cheng's Thirteen Chapters on T'ai Chi Ch'üan* by Zheng Manqing (Cheng Man-Ch'ing) and the short texts, some at least a century old, generally recognized as expressing the essence of taijiquan, and known as the *Taijiquan Classics*.[2] A literature survey of the field of taijiquan also turned up a huge number of superficial introductions in European languages, some more substantial accounts of personal experience, a few useful translations or adaptations from the Chinese, and the historical research in Chinese of Gu Luxin, Tang Hao, and Matsuta Takimoto.

Another work, Chen Xin's *Chenshi Taijiquan Tujie* (*Illustrated Explanations of Chen-Style Taijiquan*), was recommended to me by both Chinese and Westerners. This book is particularly associated with the Chen family transmission of taijiquan and discusses the art's conceptual background. First published in 1931 or 1933,[3] but written between 1908 and 1919 (later date given in the author's preface), the work seemed to be a promising source of abstruse philosophy with its multitude of abstract yin-yang diagrams.

However, as my research progressed, the *Illustrated Explanations of Chen-Style Taijiquan* appeared more problematic. Many writers on taijiquan referred to the book, and several credited it as valuable for the study of taijiquan.[4] However, none ventured any explicit interpretation of what apparently was a profound exposition of taijiquan's conceptual framework. It seemed that the *Illustrated Explanations* was not merely imposing but also intimidating, and somewhat obscure.

Some twenty years ago, a doctoral thesis entitled *Tai-ki K'iuan: Technique de Longue Vie, Technique de Combat*[5] included translations into French of some texts from Chen Xin's book (Despeux, 1976; 1981). Even that author, French sinologist Catherine Despeux, did not give an overall account of the work but gave the most attention to the sections listing postures, sequences, and the paths that the *qi* (vital energy) takes through the body in taijiquan practice. While Dr. Despeux's later research covers corporal and meditation practices other than taijiquan, she was able to inform me that current doctoral research by a Chen-style practitioner Jean-Pierre Bonpied (under the direction of Professor François Jullien at Paris VII) was addressing some of the Chen Xin texts that interested me, namely those dealing with body-mind and micro-macrocosmic connections. Mr. Bonpied was kind enough to supply me with a summary of his research, which helped in my selection of texts from Chen Xin's book for my own study.

Overview of the Book's Contents

Though my own research focused on just a few pages of the philosophical texts, I include here a brief summary of the contents of the *Illustrated Explanations of Chen-Style Taijiquan*, which appears to be a heterogeneous compilation rather than an original synthesis. The first and most imposing section, which had initially attracted my interest, constitutes some seventy pages (vol. 1, pp. 17–87) of philosophical discussion and graphic representations of the *Taiji* (Supreme Ultimate).

The subsequent forty-four pages of the *Illustrated Explanations* (pp. 97–140) detail qi circulation in an orthodox account of the traditional medical theory used in acupuncture, moxa, or *qigong* (energy work), information that was all widely available early this century when Chen Xin was writing. While perhaps unfamiliar to the Western eye, this section makes little direct contribution to an understanding of taijiquan itself.

Chen Xin does mention briefly martial applications of qi circulation theory, but without explicit detail. For example, he gives the "classic eight intersections of the meridians," mentioning that the meridians can be blocked by an attack to these points, and that the time of the attack is significant. Dr. Chen Shing-pok, a Chinese acupuncturist working in Hôpital St. Louis in Paris, and who is also a Chen-style practitioner, was able to shed some light on this vague reference. In Chinese medical theory, the different organs correspond with set hours of the day, and each organ has its own meridians. At a said hour, an attack can thus target the meridian corresponding to the organ then dominant in the body: thus in a midday combat while the heart is dominant, the heart meridian might be attacked.

Did Chen Xin hesitate to publish explicitly such dangerous techniques? He does include (juan shou, pp. 137–140) the traditional list of "mortal points" or "vulnerable points" (*dianxue*). These points are well known to martial artists, who protect them, for example, by preventing the opponent from touching the central axis of their bodies (front and rear), and thus protecting their two main meridians.

Whereas Chen Xin does not explicitly link meridian theory to martial application, his book does go on to set out another theory concerning the movement of energy in the body. In this case it is the spiraling *nei jing* (internal force) or *tan jing* (elastic force) that accumulates and uncoils like a spring. *Chansijing*, Chen Xin's formulation that the Chen Family tradition subsequently adopted, alludes to the coiled silk (*chansi*) of a cocoon. Some contemporary practitioners consider this spiraling aspect of jing important for understanding and training the jing. For example, some seek to strengthen the jing by training the *yi* (intention) along such spiraling paths before following on with the physical movement. With its

From old Chen-style first routine: transition from
Double Gusts Penetrate the Ears to Kick with Left Heel.

diagrams, Chen Xin's book provides the most explicit account of this spiraling characteristic, with an overview (juan I, pp. 92–94) and applications to particular movements (e.g., juan II, pp. 16 and 27).

The most voluminous part of the book gives detailed and illustrated instructions for the new style (*xinjia*) Chen individual form. The movements are divided into thirteen groups, symbolizing the Five Elements and Eight Trigrams (vol. I, pp. 172–174). The postures are also described in their correspondence to the sixty-four hexagrams of the *Book of Changes* (*Yijing*).

The Illustrated Explanations of Chen-Style Taijiquan ends with some ten pages of biographical and genealogical material that documents and promotes the Chen taijiquan tradition. These annals celebrate the Chen ancestors' martial prowess, rectitude, and loyalty to the government. For example, the pages devoted to Chen Zhongshen (1809–1871), Chen Xin's father, seem to be the product of filial exaggeration, and were omitted from the 1991 Xi'an edition.[6]

Extrinsic Motivations for Chen Xin's Synthesis of Philosophy & Family Boxing

I soon discovered that Chen Xin's interest in philosophy was more established than his credentials as a taijiquan practitioner. Indeed, one Wu stylist, Wu Tunan, has had no hesitation in dismissing Chen Xin's work as irrelevant and purely theoretical speculation. In his *Taijiquan Zhi Yanjiu*, Wu (1986: 51) quotes at length a meeting he says the two men had in 1917 (some sixty-five years previous). Chen Xin, then a village schoolmaster, spoke of his regret that his father had made him an academic, unlike his elder brother(s) and his cousins who were able to study boxing and became heroes in the local militia. In fairness, one must note that Wu Tunan tends to minimize the contribution of the Chen clan transmission to the taijiquan's overall development. Within the Chen tradition, however, Chen Xin is generally acknowledged as a skilled practitioner and is credited with disciples in the "genealogies" of taijiquan transmission (Chen, Z. 1991: 9).

However sincere his interest in philosophy and in Chen-style boxing, Chen Xin's melding of the two probably also reflects a concern for "face," both in terms of family prestige and in terms of his own role within his clan. Competition with his clan from the flourishing rival Yang school and his own exclusion (however partial) from the martial prowess that forged his family's identity were both factors encouraging him to validate his family's art. He did this by attempting a detailed synthesis of the martial art of taijiquan and the scholarly art of philosophy.

Throughout the second half of the nineteenth century, the popularity of Yang-style taijiquan had grown steadily, and it was even taught at the Manchu imperial court (Liao, 1990: 13–14). The founder of this style, Yang Luchan, also known as Yang Fukui (1799–1872), had served the Chen family and studied for several years with the Chen-style master Chen Changxing (1771–1853).[7]

According to one source (Ly, 1990: 89–90), it may even have been Yang who, abandoning the earlier names of "supple boxing" (*ruan quan*) and "transformation boxing" (*huaquan*), first adopted the name "taijiquan" (supreme ultimate boxing) after studying Wang Zongyue's *Taijiquan Jing* (*Taijiquan Classic*).[8] As Yang's sons and grandson also became well-known figures in the martial arts world, Chen Xin's use of the term "taijiquan" in the title and the body of his book might thus have reintegrated into the older Chen boxing the newer Yang branch. More importantly, the ancient term "taiji", which appeared in an appendix to the *Yijing* (*Book of Changes*) perfectly suited his project of harmonizing boxing techniques with *Yijing* principles.

Chen-style Left Separate Base.

Surprises in Terminology and Authorship

As I deciphered the few pages of classical Chinese I had selected, I realized that in Chen Xin's text the term "taiji" was no longer the *Book of Changes* symbol of the integration of yin and yang but was synonymous with the Neo-Confucian's Principle (*li*) and the Way (*dao*). Moreover the term "qi" was used with a meaning different from that of "vital energy" current in medicine or taijiquan practice. This is generally thought of as an energy current circulating within the body and supporting life and health as well as body movement in taijiquan.

Qi was used here in the wider sense of basic energy (or "matter-energy") which makes up all things, opposed to Principle (*li*), the innate organization of all things, both animate and inanimate, and is generally opposed to Principle (*li*), the innate organization of all things. This classic Neo-Confucianist opposition suggested that one immediate philosophical frame of reference was the Neo-Confucianist synthesis of the Song Dynasty (960–1279): an attempt to integrate Daoist cosmological concepts within the socio-ethical Confucianist tradition.

The incongruity of this conceptual framework with my expectations of taijiquan as a "Daoist practice" only made sense once I realized that the texts in question did not deal with taijiquan at all, and were not, in fact, written by Chen Xin. Catherine Despeux had noted in her thesis (1976: 30–2) that the main spiral representation of the taiji in Chen Xin's book[9] occurs in a diagram in a late Ming Dynasty (1368–1644) edition of Shao Yong's (1011–77) *Huangji Jingshi Shu* (*Book of Cosmological Chronology*), and that in both cases the representation is attributed to Lai Zhide (1525–1604). However, when I consulted a copy of Lai Zhide's own *Lai Zhu Yijing Tujie* (*Lai's Compilation of Illustrated Explanations of the Book of Changes*), I discovered that Chen Xin owes a great deal more than a single diagram to Lai Zhide (Lai, 1969). The very seventy-page section of Chen's book that had most intrigued me is almost entirely taken directly from Lai's work, a book which according to Larry Schultz (1982) was an extremely popular, though never officially endorsed text for *Yijing* scholars throughout the Qing Dynasty (1644–1911). Moreover, these texts are duly attributed to Lai in Chen's book by the annotation *"Lai Chu"* (Lai's Compilation).

If the philosophical discussion in Chen Xin's book was not the author's, can it still be thought to contribute to an understanding of his martial art? To what extent does Lai's sixteenth-century explanation of taiji shed light on the twentieth-century practice of taijiquan? Such questions required a clarification of the different conceptual frameworks appealed to in the two cases.

Chen-style Right Separate Base.

Interpreting the Term Taiji

In Professor Robinet's survey of the meaning of the expression "taiji" in pre-Ming Daoist sources (1990: 373–411),[10] it appears that aside from references to the taiji as a high divinity or as the pole star (and thus the pivot and center of the universe), this concept often acts as hinge between the One and the Many, origin and unfolding, Non-Being (*wu*) and Being (*you*). These relationships are foreshadowed in the classic formulation of the *Great Appendix* (*Xici*) to the *Book of Changes*: "The *Yi* has its Taiji, and the Taiji gives birth to the two principles [Yin and Yang]."[11] The Taiji thus is set between the Absolute (of potential to change) of the *Yi* and Relativity (of change) of yin and yang. Similarly, the fourth-century BCE book *Zhuangzi* and the second-century BCE *Huainanzi* placed the Taiji after the absolute Dao which in *Laozi* gives birth to the One, which gives birth to Two, and thus the many (Henricks, 1989: 106).

Speculating on the mechanisms of the cosmos, the Daoists integrated the Taiji into their evolutionary series of Five Geneses (*wutai*, the Five Greats) from primary chaotic and indistinguishable unity to the universe of the differentiated myriad things. Both composite and origin of the Two (yin and yang), the Taiji encapsulates the concepts of burgeoning division and return to the One.

Because of this role as hinge between One and the Many, it is no surprise that the Daoist Taiji is often preceded (logically even if not temporally) by an absolute, the *Wuji* (Ultimateless) characterized as empty, spontaneous, tangible.

Such Daoist interpretations of the Taiji and Wuji were no doubt enriched by the interest and metaphysical scope given these notions by some of the Song Dynasty Neo-Confucianists,[12] if only by the controversy and reflection these authors stimulated. Later, the writings of Zhu Xi (1130–1200), which constituted the official orthodoxy studied by Chinese scholars for six hundred years, characterized the Taiji as identical to Principle, and elsewhere as identical to the Wuji (Ultimateless). Thus the Taiji gradually took on the role of absolute for the Neo-Confucianists, giving them a totem as prestigious as the Dao of the Daoists.

In his re-evaluation of Zhu Xi orthodoxy, Lai Zhide reinstated the primacy of the *Wuji* (Ultimateless) over the *Taiji* (Supreme Ultimate): he represented the former by an empty circle, like some of his Daoist predecessors, and the Taiji by a black and white spiral with the same "empty circle" in its center. This is the relation between the two terms that is adopted by Chen Xin, who presents taijiquan as an intermediary and means of access from the ordinary world of the Myriad Things to the absolutes of Principle (*li*) and Wuji. Lai's symbol now frequently appears as a symbol for Chen-style taijiquan schools.[13]

Yijing Commentary in the Daoist and Confucianist Tradition and Relevance to Taijiquan Practice

Both Daoist and Confucian traditions see value in "a good life," but their goals are rather different. Daoists tend to take a high ethical standard as a necessary but not sufficient condition for harmonizing with the Universe or achieving personal immortality. For Confucianists (and Neo-Confucianists), personal moral development is both the duty and the destiny of humanity. One much quoted phrase from the *Book of Changes* summed up this challenge: "Exhaust Principle and plumb the depths of Nature in order to reach Heavenly Destiny" (Chen, 1991: 62).

The *Book of Changes* was popular in both Daoist and Confucianists circles. Daoism has tended to focus on the patterns of change to better understand and harmonize with the workings of the universe, while Confucianist commentary has interpreted the examples and images in the book as ethical teachings. Of course, in practice, these two, with Buddhism (the other main Chinese socio-religious tradition), have interpenetrated and enriched each other constantly.

The ideal of human development adopted by Lai Zhide, who spent some thirty years in solitary ascetic meditation on the *Book of Changes*, was self-alignment with Human Nature or Principle by dominating and eliminating self-centered desires. An illustrated analysis of the patterns of change in the stars, moon, and earth, matched with the cycle of sixty-four hexagrams in the *Book of Changes*, is presented as the heavenly model of non-egotistical conduct human beings should emulate to achieve their destiny.

While the Lai Zhide texts provide elements of an ethical and cosmological framework that includes Neo-Confucianist as well as Daoist references, these elements are *compatible with rather than specific to* the art of taijiquan, which aims at harmonious development of the physical, mental, and (for some) spiritual capacities of human beings. The links between Lai Zhide's vision and the taijiquan training system are superficially reinforced in Chen Xin's book by the similarities of terminology; such similarities actually conceal different conceptual frameworks. However, in the short texts I studied, two aspects did seem relevant to the taijiquan practitioner's moral and spiritual growth: 1) the idea of banishing a sense of self as separate from the Universe, and 2) the central role given to the human heart/mind (*ren-xin*) as the connecting agent between gross and subtle energies in the cosmos as well as in the individual.

Conclusion

Whereas Chen Xin's book is hardly satisfying as a coherent synthesis of metaphysical and martial art, his attempt to contribute to the literary tradition of taijiquan has certainly met with recognition, and has helped establish the role of the Chen clan as central in the history of taijiquan. In the sixty-five years that separate us from the publication of this work, no other author in the field has made a more ambitious attempt.

Glossary		Chinese Authors	
Chen Pai Taijiquan	陳氏太极拳	Chen Xin	陳鑫
dao	道	Chen Zhenglei	陳正雷
li	理	Lai Zhide	來知德
taiji	太極	Qiao Biao	喬㠟
wuji	無極	Liu Ronggan	劉榮淦
		Tang Hao	唐豪
		Wang Xi'an	王西安
		Wu Tunan	吳圖南

Notes

1 This research was made within the academic structure of a master's program at the University of Aix-en-Provence, supervised by Professor Isabelle Robinet, a specialist in Daoism.

2 Danny Vercammen (1994) has attempted to catalogue the variations of the Chinese texts in *Neiji Wushu: The Internal School of Chinese Martial Arts, Vol. 1*.

3 The *Zhunguo Wushu Da Cidian* (Wu, 1990: 503) cites 1931 as the first publication date of Chen Xin's *Chenshi Taijiquan Tujie*. Dufresne and Nguyen (1994: 29) mention 1931 as the year when the Henan Martial Arts Academy director bought the manuscript and give 1933 as the year of its first publication.

4 The *Zhunguo Wushu Da Cidian* lists it as "one of the most important works on taijiquan" (Wu, 1990: 503). Huang writes that Chen's book is "a secret ancient text preserved at Chen Chi Kou, Honan, . . ." (Huang, 1973: 48).

5 Catherine Despeux's 1976 academic work was revised for the general reader and republished in 1981.

6 See Hu (1993 a-b; August 1993) for a translation of a hand-copied extract of the official family history and for a discussion of the unreliability of Chen Xin's and other's accounts.

7 Rivalry and conservation of family prestige are of course still current in the martial arts world. A recent edition of Chen Xin's work (*Chen Shi Taijiquan Tushou*, Xi'an, 1991), in a passage on page 380 dealing with Chen Changxing's numerous students, omits the sentence "Yang Fukui was the most famous of them" found in the Taipei edition (Chen, 1970: 214).

8 Apparently discovered in 1852, this text may be the oldest to use the term *taijiquan*, which appeared in the title. Within the text, "taiji" is found as a philosophical term.

9 This taiji diagram appears on pages 17, 20, 21, 63, 65, 70, 78, and 80 of Chen Xin's book.

10 The present paragraph and the following three paragraphs are based on Professor Robinet's article (1990).

11 This formulation is taken from the *Zhou Yi* (*Book of Changes*) (ch. III, section 10, p. 62), found in *Si Shu Wu Jing, vol. I*.

[12] Two authors in particular, Zhou Dunyi (1017–1073) and Shao Yong, both of whom had links with Daoism and indeed Buddhism, used the term Taiji to connect the One with the Myriad Things through the evolutions of yin and yang. In his *Illustrated Explanation of Taiji* (*Taiji Tushou*), Zhou integrated the Five Elements (*wuxing*) system; while in his *Book of Cosmological Chronology*, Shao Yong assimilated the Eight Trigrams (*bagua*) system.

[13] I have not come across earlier uses of this particular symbol.

Bibliography
Works in English and French

Chen, B. (1995). A recollection of the book san san liu quan pu. *Journal of the Chenstyle Research Association*, 3: 19–21.

Cheng, M. (1982). *Master Cheng's thirteen chapters on tai chi ch'üan*. (Wile, D., Trans.). New York: Sweet Ch'i Press.

Despeux, C. (1981). *Taiji quan: Art martial, technique de longue vie*. Paris: Guy Trédaniel.

Despeux, C. (1976). *Tai-ki k'iuan: Technique de longue vie, technique de combat*. Paris: Mémoires de l'Institute des Hautes Etudes Chinoises, vol. III, Collége de France.

Dufresne, T., & Nguyen, J. (1994). *Taiji quan: Art martial de la famille Chen*. Paris: Editions Budostore.

Feng, Z. & Feng, D. (1984). *Chen Style Taijiquan*. Hong Kong: Hai Feng Publishing Co.

Fung, Y. (1983). *A history of Chinese philosophy*. (Bodde, D., Trans.). Princeton: Princeton University Press.

Henricks, R. (1989). *Lao-tzu te-dao ching*. New York: Ballintine Books.

Hu, W. (June 1993a). Ch'en-shih chia-p'u translated with commentaries. *Journal of the Chenstyle Taijiquan Research Association*, 1(3): 1–6.

Hu, W. (June 1993b). Ch'en Chung-sheng and the problem of sources, part 1. *Journal of the Chenstyle Taijiquan Research Association*, 1(3): 7–18.

Hu, W. (August 1993). Ch'en Chung-sheng and the problem of sources, part 2. *Journal of the Chenstyle Taijiquan Research Association*, 1(4): 4–16.

Huang, W. (1973). *Fundamentals of t'ai-chi ch'uan*. Hong Kong: South Sky Book Company.

Jacobs, A. (Dir.). (1990). *Encyclopédie philosophique universelle, vol. II*. Paris: Presses Universitaires de France.

Jou, T. (1980). *The tao of tai-chi chuan, way to rejuvenation*. Warwick, NY: Tai Chi Foundation.

Kelly, P. (1994). *Tai ji secrets*. (no location given): G&H Publications.

Kleinman, S. (Ed.). (1986). *Mind and body east meets west, big ten body of knowledge symposium series, vol. 15*. Champaign, IL: Human Kinetics Publishers.

Liao, W. (1990). *Tai chi classics*. Boston: Shambhala Publications Inc.

Lo, B., Inn, M., Amacker, R. & Foe, S. (1979). *Essence of t'ai chi ch'uan: The literary tradition*. Berkeley: North Atlantic Books.

Ly, A. (1990). *L'art du tai ji quan, le dao et le qi*. Paris: Lierre et Coudrier.

Ni, H. (1983). *The book of changes and the unchanging truth*. Malibu, CA: Shrine of the Eternal Breath of Tao.

Robinet, I. (1991). *Histoire du taoïsme des origines au xive siécle*. Paris: Editions du Cerf.

Robinet, I. (1990). The place and meaning of the notion of taiji in Taoist sources prior to the Ming dynasty. (Wissing, P., Trans.). *History of Religions, 29*(4): 373–411.

Schultz, L. (1982). *Lai Chih-te (1525–1604) and the phenomenology of the "Classic of Change."* Ann Arbor: University Microfilms International.

Seidel, A. (1970). A Taoist immortal of the Ming dynasty: Chang San-feng. In *Self and Society in Ming Thought*. (deBary, W., Ed.). New York: Columbia University Press.

Vercammen, D. (1994). *Neijia wushu: The internal school of Chinese martial arts, vol. I.* Gent, Belgium: Rijksuniversiteit.

Wang, P. & Zheng, W. (1983). *Wu style taijiquan: A detailed course for health and self-defence and teaching of three masters in Beijing.* Hong Kong: Hai Feng Publishing Co.

Yang, J. (1991). *Advanced Yang style tai chi chuan, vol. I.* Jamaica Plain, MA: Yang's Martial Arts Association Publication Centre.

Works in Chinese

Chen, X. (1970). *Chenshi taijiquan tujie* (Illustrated explanations of Chen Style Taijiquan). (Hua, Y., Ed.). Taipei: Hualianguan Chubanshe.

Chen, X. (1991). *Chenshi taijiquan tushuo* (Chen Style Taijiquan illustrated and explained). (Xiao, P., Ed.). Xi'an: Sanqin Chubanshe.

Chen, Z. (1991). *Chenshi taijiquan xiehui zong* (Chen Style Taijiquan association's ancestors). Xi'an: Gaodeng Jioyu Chubanshe.

Lai, Z. (1969). *Lai zhu Yijing tujie* (Lai's compilation of illustrated explanations of the *Book of Changes*). Taipei: Yiqun Chubanshe.

Matsuta, T. (1984). *Zhongguo wushu shilüe* (Chinese martial arts biographical sketch). Chongqing: Siquan Kexue Dixue Chubanshe.

Qiao, B. & Liu, R. (1990). *Jing gong Chenshi taijiquan* (Force work in Chen Style Taijiquan). Beijing: Beijing Tiyu Xueyuan Chubanshe.

Tang, H. (1963). *Taijiquan genyuan*. (The origins of taijiquan). Hong Kong: Bailing Chubanshe.

Wang, X. (1993). *Chenshi taijiquan laojia*. (Chen Style Taijiquan old style). Zhengzhou: Henan Kexue Jishu Chubanshe.

Wu, T. (1986). *Taijiquan zhi yanjiu*. (Taijiquan research). Hong Kong: Shangwu Chubanshe.

Wu, T. (1990). *Zhongguo wushu da cidian*. (Great dictionary of Chinese martial arts). Beijing: Renmin Tiyu Chubanshe.

Overlapping Steps:
Traditional Training Methods
in Chen Village Taijiquan

by David Gaffney, B.A.

The author performing a Chen-style
taijiquan movement called Hidden Fist.
All photographs courtesy of David Gaffney.

Introduction

Though many people can quote the requirements of taijiquan and verses from the taijiquan classics, real understanding can only come through training. According to Chen Fake, the style's 17th-generation standard-bearer, those learning taijiquan must not only appreciate the theories intellectually, they must also train the methods into their body. Theoretical knowledge should be accompanied by practical action: "How much you accomplish depends entirely on how much effort you put in" (Ma Hong, 1988: 13). In his *Illustrated Explanation of Chen Family Taijiquan* (1986), Chen Xin goes further, suggesting that "all that idle talk does is to create a tide of black ink; actually putting it into practice is the real thing" (Gaffney & Sim, 2000: 94).

Chen taijiquan requires the body to be used in a unique, disciplined way and has a wide-ranging training curriculum encompassing standing exercises, single-movement exercises, bare-hand forms, push-hands, weapons, and supplementary equipment training. In common with other sports or martial arts, it is essential

43

to begin with the basics. With time and conscientious practice, the body is strengthened and one discovers a new way of moving. Each of the different training methods should be viewed within the framework of a larger system. Each facet of training, from the standing exercises to advanced push-hands drills, is interconnected and necessary. Considered in its entirety, the training process can be likened to a series of overlapping steps, each laid upon the underpinning foundation of the preceding one.

In Chenjiagou, it is commonly stated that all practice must be done "according to the principles" (Gu & Shen, 1998: 306). The principles start with the fundamental requirements and progress incrementally to the highest skill levels. Developing correct habits is a gradual process and the key to traditional training is to have patience en route to acquiring competence.

In the West, people often think of taijiquan as an easy option. Chenjia villagers, however, have long understood that learning taijiquan is often painstaking and arduous. The Chen taijiquan student begins by seeking to understand and manage essential body requirements and execute basic body movements. Training is focused upon developing sufficient internal as well as external strength to carry out these actions rather than being impatient for the more complex techniques.

Street sign showing the way to Chen Village.

Standing Pole — Entering the Door

Chen Xin's *Illustrated Explanation of Chen Family Taijiquan* (1986) suggests that: "To train *taiji*, one must begin at *wuji*" (quiet, nothingness). This provides the guideline for entering the door of Chen taijiquan's traditional training curriculum. Standing pole (*zhan zhuang*) is the most basic taijiquan exercise and is common to many Chinese martial arts. Typically, the arms are held in front of the body as if holding a large ball as the practitioner stands and quietly observes the natural ebb and flow of the breath. The standing pole exercise, however, can be practiced using any of the end postures from the taiji form. During "standing practice, a static posture is maintained for a period of time, with emphasis upon developing awareness of and maintaining the most efficient and relaxed structural alignment necessary to hold the position.

To the casual observer, it may appear as if little is happening. The experienced practitioner, though, is intensely engaged in a variety of actions and sensations. Prolonged practice of this ostensibly uncomplicated exercise, along with enhancing postural awareness and calmness of mind, significantly increases leg strength. When the legs are strong and can bear weight securely, then the upper body can relax and sink down into them, making the top more flexible. If the legs do not have sufficient strength, the top is "afraid" to sink down, and the body remains top heavy and tense. All Chen taijiquan training methods look to develop extreme lightness and sensitivity in the upper body. Simultaneously, the lower body should exhibit a feeling of extreme heaviness and connection to the ground. At this stage, the practitioner can be said to be putting down roots. The importance of this is reflected in the verse "Cultivate the roots and the branches and leaves will be abundant" (Gaffney & Sim, 2000: 132).

November 2004 Intensive Training Camp organized by Chen Taiji Great Britain. Back row, left to right: Yaniv Morada (Israel), Neill Baker (UK), Fabrizio Cuminetti (Italy). Front: Riger Twigg (UK), Gabrilla Morgado (Portugal), Davidine Siaw-Voon Sim (UK), Chen Xiaoxing, David Gaffney (UK), and Chen Zhiqiang.

Taijiquan is an internal martial art, entailing internal energy (*nei jing*) training in addition to external physical training. The power and strength of internal energy are manifested in external actions. To train internal skills, one must first train the body's intrinsic energy (*qi*). This includes cultivation, storage, and circulation of qi. Standing pole practice provides a means of increasing internal feeling and qi circulation. Regular standing for extended periods gives rise to acute body awareness as the practitioner learns to relax and sink their qi. By reducing the level of external stimulation, one can focus more closely upon sensations within the body. While the external body is still, internally the breath, blood, and qi are circulating. This represents a state of balance, or "motion in stillness."

A demonstration by members of the
Chen Village Taijiquan School in the
memorial ground of Chen Wangting.

Through prolonged training, qi becomes fuller and stronger, filling the energy center in the lower abdomen (*dantian*), breaking through blockages in the energy paths (*jingluo*), and then saturating the whole body. The body is like an inflated ball, full of elasticity and overflowing with a physical sensation of inward to outward expansion and strength (*peng jing*). With Chen taijiquan's spiraling silk-reeling movement, this energy can be circulated throughout the body.

The standing pole training requirements are carried over to the taiji form: head erect, shoulders relaxed, elbows sunk down, chest relaxed, hips sunk, knees bent, etc. To correctly follow these basic and seemingly simple principles requires deep concentration. As one develops competence in the different aspects during standing, the feelings and sensations that arise can be transferred to the taiji form and push-hands.

The Chen Village Taijiquan School.

Left: Statue of Chen Changxing.
Right: Practicing the old frame first routine,
Golden Rooster Standing on One Leg.

Empty-Hand Forms: The Foundation of Chen Taijiquan Skills

Form training has long provided the foundation of Chen taijiquan's step-by-step training method. Chen Wangting's original art was comprised of five empty-hand boxing routines that were passed down the next five generations. Chen Changxing (1771–1853), the 14th-generation standard bearer, refined the five routines into the two routines practiced today. These are the first routine (*yilu*) and the second routine (*erlu*, also known as the *Paochui* or Cannon Fist form).

It has been suggested that some of Chen Wangting's unique art was lost. Chen Xiaoxing, principal of the Chenjiagou Taijiquan School, refutes this: "The synthesis of the five routines was not a matter of losing the old forms but of putting the five together, absorbing the essence of each. The first routine and the Cannon Fist contain the same essence as the original routines, preserving many of the movements and all of the movement principles" (Chen Xiaoxing, 2004). Today, Chen-style taijiquan empty-hand forms consist of two main versions (frames): old and new (*laojia* and *xinjia*, respectively). The old frame has been handed down relatively unchanged since Chen Changxing's time, while 17th-generation master Chen Fake developed the new frame. The new frame incorporates more obvious silk-reeling movement, more power releasing actions, and greater emphasis on joint-locking (*qinna*) techniques. Each consists of a first routine and Cannon Fist. Where the first routine is characterized by slow, soft movements, the second is predominantly fast and powerful.

Chen Xiaoxing at practice —
certain optimum patterns of movement must
be established and these can only become
set if they are repeated almost endlessly.

It is important to understand form training within the context of a larger system. Nowadays, people often equate knowing many forms with martial expertise. Adam Hsu (1998: 93) cautions that we should not confuse quantity with quality arguing: "Students who spend their time learning multitudes of forms are wasting their time. This kind of practice, void of a true foundation, is no more than folk dance" because "each form has its own purpose and each form is one step in a clear progression of training."

In the beginning, the student should seek to standardize movement as far as possible in accordance to Chen taijiquan's basic requirements for each part of the body. Each of the requirements has practical implications for maintaining good health, for maximizing movement efficiency, for qi circulation, and for heightening martial effectiveness.

Primary emphasis is placed upon understanding the underlying movement principles and then progressing to standardized movement. Once this is accomplished, the next goal is to search for further realization of the internal circulation of energy. When you first come to the fixed postures, for example, lazily tying coat or Single Whip, in your mind you must very stringently adjust yourself according to the requirements for each part of the body. Everyone knows the requirements as they have been widely written about, it is the degree that is hard to realize. For instance, all experienced taijiquan practitioners are familiar with the requirement to "store the chest" (*han xiong*), but how do you store? If you store too much, the waist collapses, but what is too much? It is not like carpentry where someone just gives you the measurements and you can do it accordingly.

Only through persistent practice and strict adherence to correct principles can one achieve a stage where one is able to produce just the right amount of *jing* [internal force], change at will, and rotate with ease. One has to train hard in form practice so that the body becomes one single unit, which enables one movement activating all movements.

– Chen Xiaowang, 1990: 29

In this context, we can understand the logic behind Chen taijiquan's traditional emphasis upon the first routine as the foundation form. The form's slower nature permits the practitioner to pay attention to details, to make certain that postures are precise, to test stability and balance during movement, to enhance lower body strength, and to become conscious of the circulation of qi throughout the body.

Herman Kauz (1989: 80) succinctly sums up the benefits of this intense attention to detail during form practice:

Individual training of this nature enables the student to grow accustomed to the body mechanics involved in the performance of his techniques. He is not distracted by an opponent's shifting about evasively or attempting to counterattack. He has time in which to work on problems concerned with correct foot placement, body position or pulling direction. In an actual match, the opportunity to perform a throw appears only briefly, allowing insufficient time to give attention to the many factors involved. Certain optimum patterns of movement must be established, and these can only become set if they are repeated almost endlessly.

As the practitioner's skill increases, they may begin training in the Cannon Fist routine to develop the explosive release of strength (*bao fali*) as well as their endurance and stamina (*nai li*). Taijiquan is built upon the model of hardness and softness complementing and alternating with each other. Consequently, the two forms represent a complete balanced system of hardness and softness. The Cannon Fist routine is physically very demanding with many instances of energy release (*fajing*), fast movements, sweeps, elbow and shoulder techniques, and sudden changes of attack and defense. Where the first routine provides the means of developing internal energy, the second is said to consolidate and express this energy (Chen Xiaoxing, 2004).

Push-Hands: To Know One's Opponent

Chen Wangting created the two-person training drill called push hands, the objective of which is to attain sensitivity to the movement and intention of an adversary while masking one's own intention and energy. Attaining this heightened level of sensitivity has long been the goal of Chen taiji exponents. In the "Song of the Canon of Boxing," Chen Wangting states that one should seek to accomplish a level of ability where: "Nobody knows me, while I know everybody" (Chen Zhenglei, 1992, Vol. 3: 1).

Harmonizing with an opponent's movements, the practitioner works toward eliminating all tension and resistance within his own responses. In contrast to most external martial arts, the intention is not just to block an incoming force with greater force, but to "listen" to and "borrow" the opponent's energy to defend oneself.

This listening skill is not solely dependent upon the sense of touch but of whole body awareness. Many people make the mistake of turning their heads to one side or closing their eyes while pushing hands. In actual fact, there must be a combination and coordination of sight, hearing, and touch; and one is not exclusive of the others.

Fabrizio Cuminetti (left) and David Gaffney pushing hands —
Single Forward and Back Step.

According to Chen Xiaowang (1990: 29), push hands and form practice are inseparable:

> Whatever shortcomings one has in the form will certainly show up as weaknesses during push hands, giving an opponent the opportunity to take advantage. To this end, one needs to practice push hands; check on the forms; understand the internal force (*jing*); and learn how to express the force (*fa-jing*) as well as how to neutralize the force (*hua ing*). If one is able to withstand confrontational push hands, then it is an indication that one has understood the underlying taiji principles. Continuous training will lead to increased confidence. At this point one can step up one's training and bring in supplementary training such as shaking the long pole; practicing with weapons such as the sabre, spear, sword, and staff; and doing single-posture training such as fajing.

Understanding the trained energies of the body (*jing*) lies at the heart of push-hands practice. Fundamental to achieving this is a careful study of taijiquan's eight methods or *ba fa*. From these eight methods or energies all skills and techniques are generated. The eight energies comprise four frontal methods (*si zheng*), which are quite familiar to most taiji practitioners: warding (*peng*); diverting (*lu*); squeezing (*ji*) and pressing down (*an*).

The next four skills, also known as the four diagonal methods (*si yu*), are less familiar: plucking (*cai*), splitting (*lie*), elbowing (*zhou*), and bumping (*kao*). Mastering these four is important if one is to acquire a true understanding of the throwing and striking that Chen taijiquan is famous for. Unlike the first four methods, *cai*, *lie*, *zhou*, and *kao* are typically instilled when the student begins practicing at higher speeds and with more force (Berwick, 2000: 191–2).

Taiji push-hands is built upon the foundation of forms practice. At this stage, the practitioner should have a good understanding of how to use their body in accordance with taijiquan's strict movement principles. Training centers on the interchange of energies between the two participants. For example, when a partner uses press down, you ward off. When he uses squeeze in, you divert away. Chen Changxing stressed the importance of painstakingly studying the different energy methods in his "Song of Pushing Hands": "Be conscientious about *peng*, *lu*, *ji*, and *an*. Following each other above and below, difficult for people to enter" (Zhu, 1994: 281).

For generations, Chen taiji boxers have sought to fulfill the push-hands principles of "connecting, joining, sticking, and following," "neither letting go nor resisting" (Wang, 1998: 10). Push-hands allows the practitioner to put to the test the body postures trained in the forms. Correct body alignment enables one to control others and yet prevent them from entering one's boundary.

Chen-style taijiquan traditionally uses five methods of push-hands:

- Wuan hua: fixed step, single- and double-handed exercises
- Ding bu: fixed step, double-handed
- Huang bu (*jin yi tui yi*): single backward/forward step, double-handed
- Da lu: moving step, low stance, double-handed
- Luang cai hua: free steps, double-handed

Beyond these is the practice of free pushing or *san tui*.

Lafcadio Hearn (1850–1904), former chair of English literature at the Imperial University of Tokyo, eloquently expressed his fascination of the Asian martial arts ideal of using sensitivity to overcome superior strength. Although he had probably never seen taiji push hands, his description of the approach to training he saw in late 18th-century Japan could have been written with it in mind:

> What Western brain could have elaborated this strange teaching—never to oppose force to force, but only to direct and utilize the power of attack; to overthrow the enemy solely by his own effort? Surely none! The occidental mind appears to work in straight lines; the oriental in wonderful curves and

circles. Yet how fine a symbolism of intelligence as a means to foil brute force!
– Hearn, 1989: 57–58

Single-Posture Training

For generations, Chen taijiquan practitioners in Chenjiagou have followed an integrated system designed to increase martial ability. The process involves form, push-hands and single-posture training and each has its unique part to play. While trained separately, the three are closely interconnected: "push-hands is the means by which the accuracy of the form can be tested; form training is the foundation upon which effective push-hands skills are built; single-posture training is the means by which martial skill is brought out" (Gaffney & Sim, 2000: 136).

"Fixing the frame" —
a young coach making
sure that students'
postures are precise.

Chen Zhaokui outlined some of the reasons single-posture practice must be included alongside the more widely seen form and push-hands training:

Some applications of the movement cannot be used in push-hands. For example elbow strikes, leg methods and also attacking vital points of an opponent, or qinna. Also some very fast fajing movements in the form cannot be done successively, as it would be too exhausting.
– Ma Hong, 1998: 21

Training the empty hand form lays the foundation upon which all
other skills are built. Children in the foreground practicing double-saber.
Many of the weapon forms have changed little since they were
formulated, providing a window on taijiquan origins.

At first sight, single-posture training may seem tiresome and repetitive.
Nonetheless, going over individual movements many times significantly increases
the capacity to use them practically. Single-posture practice often focuses on building effective *fajing* ability. Even so, there should be no departure from taijiquan's
core principles. Any movement where force is emitted must be characterized by
looseness, pliability, and elasticity, rather than rigidity and stiffness. Just because
a movement is fast and powerful, does not mean the practitioner should lose sight
of the need to follow the silk-reeling spiral path rather than straight-line movement (Ma Hong, 1998: 400).

Single-movement practice can be divided into several different groups, beginning with those actions performed while stationary. Examples in the old frame
first routine include the stamping movement that concludes the Buddha's Warrior Attendant Pounds Mortar, the Hidden Thrust Punch, and the Green Dragon
Out of the Water. Other single movements embrace those that entail stepping,
for instance, stepping forward using *fajing* while training the energy methods of
taijiquan (e.g. *cai, lie, zhou, kao*), and retreating movements, as in the posture step
back and whirl arms.

Short Weapons Training

Weapons training has always played an important part in the Chen curriculum. At the time of its creation, Chen taijiquan was practiced essentially to develop the Chenjiagou villagers' martial and military skills. Without a doubt, the

training would have greatly enhanced the taiji boxers' health, but this was not the main reason for practicing the art. In Chen Wangting's day, guns had yet to appear, traditional weapons were still being carried onto the battlefield and used in combat.

Today, most people consider the weapon routines of the assorted Chinese martial arts only from the perspective of demonstrating or exercising in the park. Viewing the Chen weapon forms in this way shows a superficial appreciation of their fundamental nature. Preserved within each of the Chen weapons routines is a complex martial training manual. As well as the flexible sinuous movements, the forms include numerous dynamic actions; swift changes in tempo; and fierce chopping, slicing, or thrusting movements.

Viewed in the light of the whole system, weapons training adds to the empty-hand training by magnifying certain requirements. For instance, the mind and intention must be extended all the way through the weapon's length; movements must stay relaxed, agile, and efficient at the same time as one controls a weighted object; and footwork must be lively and responsive to permit rapid changes in the fighting sequence. Within the Chen training curriculum, numerous weapons are still practiced, including sword (*jian*), broadsword (*dao*), spear (*qiang*), halberd (*guandao*, often rendered *quandao* or *kwando*), pole, double sword, double broadsword, and double iron mace.

The sword is one of the oldest weapons in Chinese martial arts history. Archaeologists have uncovered swords from as far back as the Bronze Age. When the terracotta army was unearthed in the early Chinese capital Xi'an, a find dating back to the Qin Dynasty more than two thousand years ago, the statues of officers were carrying swords (Tian & Zhen, 2004: 102).

The Chen taijiquan sword is generally light in weight, with a flexible blade. For the Chen taiji swordsman, success on the battlefield depended upon skill, precision, and speed. Chen taijiquan contains one single straight sword form consisting of forty-nine postures. In his book *Chen Family Taiji*, Chen Zhenglei (1997: 217) explains:

> The forty-nine postures can be sub-divided into thirteen basic techniques: thrusting downward (*zha*), level or upward thrust (*ci*), pointing by flicking the wrist (*dian*), chopping (*pi*), slicing levelly or obliquely upward (*mo*), sweeping (*sao*), neutralizing in a circular path (*hua*), circular deflection with point uppermost (*liao*), hanging (*gua*), pushing up (*tuo*), pushing (*tui*), intercepting (*jie*), and raising the opponent's weapon overhead (*jia*).

The sword's flexibility allows the proficient swordsman to inflict injury from a great range of angles utilizing many diverse techniques. Its great versatility has led to the saying that there is "no gap the sword cannot enter, and no gap that another can enter" (Chen Zhenglei, 1992, Vol. 1: 180).

The different weapons help to train the many diverse qualities essential in honing a "taijiquan physique." Practicing the Chen sword form allows an exponent to develop the ability to project energy in a relaxed manner to the sword tip. It also helps to create an efficient taiji body, with repeated practice loosening the large joints such as the hips and shoulders, as well as helping to increase the suppleness of the wrists and hands.

In Chen taijiquan, the sword used is generally
light in weight, with a flexible blade.

Easily distinguishable from the sword, which is double edged and light, the broadsword is single edged and heavy. The broadsword's strength led to cutting movements that are large, expansive, and powerful. In appearance, using the broadsword is said to be "like splitting a mountain." In character, the broadsword is traditionally compared to a ferocious tiger, with each movement being more direct and easily understandable than the straight sword. This is reflected in the Chinese martial arts saying "*Dao*—like a fierce tiger; *jian*—like a Swimming Dragon" (Chen Zhenglei, 1997, Vol. 1: 217).

The Chen broadsword form is short and dynamic. Although classified as a short weapon, the broadsword can cover a surprisingly long distance by utilizing explosive leaping and jumping movements. Movements can be performed in different ways depending upon the ultimate objective of practice. Often the routine is executed with long, low stances as a way of conditioning the body, increasing one's power and speed.

As a means of overall body training, the explosive leaping and jumping movements have much in common with modern plyometric exercises used by many of today's elite sports performers. Simply put, the combination of speed and strength is power. For many years, coaches and athletes have sought to improve power to enhance performance. Throughout the last century and no doubt long before, jumping, bounding, and hopping exercises have been used in various ways to enhance athletic performance. In recent years, this distinct method of training for power or explosiveness has been termed plyometrics (Flach, 2005: 14). In Chenjiagou, taijiquan exponents have long understood this method of training to enhance the individual's explosive actions.

Using very low stances, however, prevents the dexterity and fleetness of footwork required in a real conflict. The taiji boxer focusing on training the applications within the broadsword routine would usually practice in a higher posture to enhance mobility. Consequently, to achieve both martial and conditioning benefits, Chenjiagou practitioners have traditionally trained over a range of heights.

Long Weapons

Chen taijiquan also has a number of weapons for long-range combat, including the halberd, long pole, and the "King of Weapons" — the spear. An often-cited phrase— "one hundred days to practice broadsword, one thousand days to practice spear" —reflects the form's intricacy and difficulty level (Chen Zhenglei, 1992, Vol. 2: 52).

Also known as the "Pear Flower Spear" and "White Ape Staff," the Chen taijiquan spear form includes the functions of both spear and staff. The routine dates back to Chen Wangting, making it one of the earliest taiji forms. In his comprehensive review of taijiquan, *The Origin, Evolution, and Development of Shadow Boxing*, Gu Liuxin cites the evidence gathered by historian Tang Hao, who concluded that the texts of famous Ming Dynasty (C.E. 1368–1644) General Qi Jiguang had a profound influence on Chen Wangting's creation of taijiquan. Qi's military training text documented the spear techniques of the Yang Family 24-Movement Spear Form. The Yang family in question refers to a renowned Song Dynasty (C.E. 960–1279) (female warrior who used the form to avenge the slaying of her male relatives, so should not be confused with the Yang taijiquan family (Gu, 1996).

The Chen taiji spear form's earliest version followed the sequence of the Yang 24-Movement form in both posture and name. Its uniqueness came as a result of the application of taiji movement principles to the existing method. In the ensuing years, the Chen spear form has increased from 24 to 72 movements, adding a variety of staff movements.

Watching a skilled exponent performing with the staff, its martial roots are immediately apparent. The overall tempo is forceful, direct and rapid, with few movements being done slowly. Although it is highly unlikely that anyone would need to use the spear for combat today, the Chen family spear form remains a highly practical training tool. Spear practice enhances empty-hand skills by improving balance through the use of intricate and rapid-stepping movements as well as developing upper body strength and overall flexibility.

Training with the *guandao*: the
favored weapon of Chen taijiquan
creator Chen Wangting.

Variously known as the Spring and Autumn Broadsword, the Green Dragon
Crescent Moon Broadsword, or simply the "Big Knife," the halberd (*ji*) is one of
the system's oldest weapons forms. Characterized by strong and powerful movements, the halberd is a large and heavy weapon requiring a high degree of upper
body strength and a stable root to manipulate it freely. The Chen taijiquan halberd
trains the practitioner to move and be responsive in every direction. The favored
weapon of Chen Wangting, it is recorded in the genealogy of the Chen Family
(Chen Zhenglei, 1999: 4), that:

> Wangting, alias Zhouting, was a knight at the end of the Ming Dynasty [C.E.
> 1368–1644] and a scholar in the early years of the Qing Dynasty [C.E.
> 1644–1912]. He was known in Shandong Province as a martial arts master,
> once defeating more than a thousand bandits. He was the originator of the
> barehanded and armed combat boxing of the Chen school. He was a born
> warrior, as can be proved by the broadsword he used in combat.

While the individual names of the weapon or empty-hand forms describe
the movements, the halberd form is unique. Each of its thirty movements is given
a seven-character song or poem. When taken in their entirety, they recount the
story of General Guan, a famous warrior from the turbulent Three Kingdoms Period (C.E. 25–220). Consequently, every time the form is practiced, his exploits
are re-enacted (Gaffney & Sim, 2000: 188).

Contemporary practitioners should not overlook the importance of the
weapons routines as they offer a tangible link to past generations.

The forms are at once practical and aesthetic. Artistically pleasing to watch, the weapons routines are physically complex and demanding to complete. Many of the weapon forms have changed little since the time of Chen Wangting. Consequently they provide a window to the origins of taijiquan and represent an important legacy to today's taijiquan practitioner.

– Gaffney & Sim, 2000: 172

Supplementary Equipment Training

Standing pole, forms practice, silk-reeling exercises, push-hands, etc., all lead to an increase in internal strength. As the practitioner reaches a more accomplished level, the use of supplementary exercises with a variety of training equipment can further amplify this energy. Skills such as neutralizing, yielding, grappling (*qinna*), and *fajing* are more efficient when backed by greater physical strength.

Past masters placed great emphasis on supplementary power training methods (*xing gong*). In Chenjiagou, in the garden where Yang Luchan, the progenitor of Yang taijiquan, is said to have learned from Chen Changxing, there is still a stone weight weighing about eighty kilograms that the two are reputed to have trained with to increase their hand strength.

Also popular to this day is the exercise of shaking a long pole as a means of increasing the power that can be transmitted from the *dantian* out to the extremities. Cut from the baila tree, the pole is typically about four yards long and roughly an inch and a half in diameter. This type of wood is flexible and springy, allowing the practitioner to transmit force through it. It is said that Chen Fake performed three hundred repetitions of this exercise daily, as well as at least thirty repetitions of the empty-hand form.

Supplementary equipment training. Chen Xiaoxing watches the author lifting a stone weight to increase hand strength.

Training starts at a young age in Chenjiagou.
A three-year-old child going through his form.

Conclusion

Chen Village taijiquan is a unique example of Chinese martial culture, providing a tangible link to past generations of taiji practitioners. Changed little through the passing generations, this art today draws increasing numbers of practitioners attracted by its characteristics of power, grace, and agility. To succeed, modern practitioners would be well advised to look to the appropriate method for their stage of development and not to be in a hurry to learn new things. Above all, practice must be patient, systematic, and persistent if advanced ability is to be attained. To quote an old Chinese proverb: "One day's chill does not result in three feet of ice" (Gaffney & Sim, 2000: 148).

Bibliography

Berwick, S. (2000). The five stages of Chen taiji combat training. In *Ultimate guide to Tai Chi: The best of Inside Kung Fu*. Chicago: McGraw-Hill/Contemporary Books.

Chen, X. (1990). *Chen Style Taijiquan transmitted through generations*. Beijing: People's Sports Publishing.

Chen, X. (2004). CTGB Interview, Nov. 2004 Chenjiagou Training Camp.

Chen, Z. (1992). *A compendium of taijiquan boxing and weapons* (Volume 1). Beijing: Higher Education Press.

Chen, Z. (1992). *A compendium of taijiquan boxing and weapons* (Volume 2). Beijing: Higher Education Press.

Chen, Z. (1992). *A compendium of taijiquan boxing and weapons* (Volume 3). Beijing: Higher Education Press.

Chen, Z. (1999). *The art of Chen family taijiquan*. Shanxi: Technical Sports Publications.

Chen, Z. (1997). *Chen family taiji: Master's insights*. Xi'an: World Books.

Flach, A. (2005). *The complete book of isometrics*. Long Island City, NY: Hatherleigh Press.

Gu, L. (1996). The origin, evolution and development of shadow boxing. In *Chen Style Taijiquan* (Feng Zhiqiang and Feng Dabiao, Eds.). Beijing: People's Sports Publishing.

Gu, L. & Shen J. (1998). *Chen Style Taijiquan*. Beijing: People's Sports Publishing.

Hearn, L. (1989). Jiujutsu. In *Martial arts reader: Classic writings on philosophy and technique*. New York: Overlook Press.

Hsu, A. (1998). *The sword polisher's record: The way of kung-fu*. Boston: Tuttle Publishing.

Kauz, H. (1989). The aim of individual form practice. In *Martial arts reader: Classic writings on philosophy and technique*. New York: Overlook Press.

Ma, H. (1998). *Chen Style Taijiquan method and theory*. Beijing: Sports University Press.

Tian, Y. & Zhen, Q. (2004). *Wondrous wushu*. Guangxi: People's Publications.

Wang, X. (1998). *Push hands skills and methods*. Henan Sports Publications.

Zhu, T. (1994). *Authentic Chenjiagou taijiquan*. Percetaken Turbo Sdn. Bhd., Malaysia.

Taiji's Chen Village Under the Influence of Chen Xiaoxing

by Stephan Berwick, M.A.*

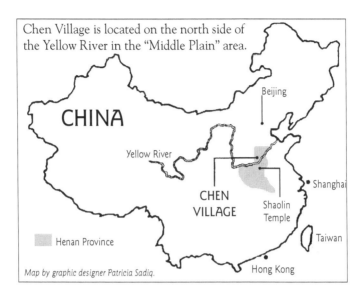

Chen Village is located on the north side of the Yellow River in the "Middle Plain" area.

Beijing

CHINA

Yellow River

CHEN VILLAGE

Shaolin Temple

Shanghai

Henan Province

Taiwan

Hong Kong

Map by graphic designer Patricia Sadiq.

Rare photo from 1985 with (from right) Chen Xiaoxing,
Chen Xiaowang, and Chen Zhenglei in front of the
Chenjiagou Training Academy. *Photos courtesy of
Stephan Berwick, Chen Xiaoxing, and Ren Guangyi.*

Introduction

Young athletes at the Chenjiagou (Chen Family Village) training academy usually begin their day with an "old-fashioned" breakfast of thick cornmeal soup, vegetables, and steamed bread. For hard-training boxers, their very large bowls of soup boast a clean, nourishing flavor that seems to fill the Chen Village boxing trainee with more than just breakfast. In this village of ancient boxers, the soup hints at the Chen Village saying, "If you drink the water in Chen Village, you will kick very well." In essence, this breakfast is a tradition that is a reminder of what fortified the early boxers of the renowned Chen Village.

The Chen Village gives the first-time visitor an infusion of both family and martial art spirit that is hard to find elsewhere. The village's houses and roads are virtually unchanged since its founding by the first Chen (nine generations ago), who settled in this gully area close to the Yellow River. Chen Village's untouched rural quality lends its boxing art a rare purity. Thus what is usually only a memory in the world of Chinese martial tradition persists in Chen Village today.

Like all traditions, assimilating a martial arts tradition requires that one step back to move forward. Although the martial art standard bearers of traditions that breed combat mastery are becoming easier to find, training under them for an extended period remains difficult. In an age of high technology, economic opportunity, and firearms, committing to a quality teacher is often impractical for most contemporary martial artists. Regardless, today's traditional martial arts enthusiast continues to seek unbroken martial traditions. In the quest to find bearers of mature martial traditions, enthusiasts can seek out the best teachers they have access to or go to the source of their martial arts discipline—if the source still exists.

Be it by design or luck, the birthplace of taijiquan remains intact. The over 400-year old village of the Chen family—in Wen County, Henan Province—is one of the few places in the world where one of the oldest and enormously influential martial traditions survives in purity. Even though some martial art researchers have questioned the exact origins of taiji, citing a lack of early martial art writings from Chen Village, its maturity and pervasiveness suggest otherwise (Wile, 1996: 117).

A normal day in Chen Village is built around farming and boxing. Boxing practice takes place everywhere: in the fields, at homes, and at the village school. However, the village school remains the nucleus of boxing training.

At the height of his teaching career, the eighteenth generation grandmaster, Chen Zhaopei, organized classes for the villagers based out of his home. His promotion and organization of taiji instruction led to the evolution of Chen Village's formal training academy, built in 1982. This sleep-in, full-time training academy has its roots in Zhaopei's original ideas. Nineteenth generation exponents remember him as the Chen family boxing master responsible for the revival of taiji practice in the village amidst the political and social upheaval of China's contemporary history (Rich, 2000).

Chen Taijiquan Standard Bearer

Chen Zhaopei's example created a new standard of leadership for the modern masters of Chen Village. At Zhaopei's urging, Chen Zhaokui—son of Chen Fake—returned to Chen Village to train the best of the nineteenth generation masters that lead the art today. Of the small group that was mentored by Chen Zhaokui, Chen Xiaoxing was one of the youngest. With Chen Zhaopei's commitment to Chen Village as inspiration, along with intimate coaching from his older brother—Chen Xiaowang, protégé of Chen Zhaokui, and the current nineteenth generation style standard bearer—Chen Xiaoxing's early training prepared him to quietly emerge as the head teacher in Chen Village.

Extremely rare group photo from 1965. First seated teenager from right, Chen Xiaowang; third from right, Chen Xiaoxing. Second row: first from right, Chen Zhaopei; fifth from right, Chen Zhaokui. Grey spot on photo is from a camera flash.

As the head boxing teacher in Chen Village, Chen Xiaoxing is not only the senior boxing master in the village, but is a community leader who commands respect. During morning and mid-day strolls with the grandmaster, the author witnessed the deference and affectionate respect accorded him. Villagers refer to him only as *shifu* (teacher) and *laoshi* (elder teacher) whenever they speak with him.

His early morning routine begins with tending to the affairs of the academy and teaching. He often ends the day with an occasional game of mahjong with village elders—often at a courtyard adjacent to the original training hall where fourteenth generation grandmaster and compiler of the old frame (*laojia*) forms, Chen Changxing, taught Yang Luchan.

Chen Xiaoxing's commitment to the village and its stable of boxers is unique in a martial arts era often dominated by legitimate masters, such as his world-renowned older brother, Chen Xiaowang, who work hard to spread their art by teaching seminars for students globally. In this vein, his older brother has done much to spread authentic Chen taijiquan. However, Chen Xiaoxing has chosen another, more traditional path to pass on the high standards of skill characteristic of Chen-style taiji boxers.

Left: Chen Xiaoxing in front of his family home.
Right: Chen Xiaoxing demonstrating punching skills.

The training hall in Chenjiagou, where
Chen Chanxing taught Yang Luchan.

Chen Xiaoxing in front of the
large Chen Family Taijiquan altar.

Wide view of the Chen family taijiquan altar with banner
celebrating the 400th birthday of Chen taiji founder, Chen Wangting.

Continuing the tradition of high technical standards built around famous
Chen taiji concepts, including the training of silk-reeling energy (*chansijing*) and
the application of the yin and yang theory, Chen Xiaoxing says: "I am inspired by
my brother to pass on a high quality art." Chen Xiaoxing not only runs the village
school, he also closely mentors the next generation of Chen taiji masters, including his nephew, Chen Xiaowang's youngest son and boxing prodigy, Chen Pengfei.

Like his elder, Chen Zhaopei, Chen Xiaoxing coaches aspiring village boxers and foreigners. Chen Xiaoxing asserts that "I am committed to remaining in
Chen Village to teach and pass on the highest quality art possible to the next generation." His commitment to teaching in the village is an example of how traditions are preserved at the source.

Left: Chen Xiaoxing demonstrating a spear form. Center and right: Chen Xiaoxing correcting and demonstrating for his nephew, Chen Pengfei, who is the youngest son of Chen Xiaowang.

The Making of a Traditional Boxing Master

Born in 1952, Chen Xiaoxing is one of only a handful of accomplished taiji masters alive today who were trained by the best of Chen taiji's legendary masters, including Chen Xiaowang, Chen Zhaopei, and his uncle, Chen Zhaokui. Chen Xiaoxing's martial arts training personifies an old Chen Village saying: "In Chen Village, by the time you're two, you can execute diamond pestle" [a classic Chen taiji technique].

Chen Xiaoxing began training at the age of six. He was first taught by his older brother, Chen Xiaowang, then Chen Zhaopei, and then again by his brother. Most of his early training was spent with just Chen Xiaowang. He describes this period, "as a peaceful, quiet time." He focused on the classic first form of Chen taiji, the old frame, first form (*laojia yilu*), averaging an astounding thirty repetitions of this long form per day. Later on, weapons and push-hands training (*tuishou*) were added to his regimen. In 1972, he started training under Chen Zhaokui, who taught him Chen Fake's new frame (*xinjia*)—Chen Fake's more detailed version of the open-hand forms.

Chen Xiaoxing related that, "Chen Zhaokui's return to Chen Village in 1964 brought much change to the villagers' practice. Zhaokui corrected mistakes and elevated their skill." Xiaoxing studied under Chen Zhaokui until 1980. Because of his young age, he then resumed his training under his brother, who became Chen Zhaokui's protégé. When Chen Xiaoxing resumed training under his then highly advanced brother, his training "became especially intense."

His training history illustrates how traditions and standards are passed in Chen Village. Fathers, elder brothers, and uncles routinely mentor the best of the next generation in public and private classes. Now open to non-Chen family members, this type of family-shared training remains intact. This openness to teaching outsiders began when seventeenth-generation grandmaster Chen Changxing taught Yang Luchan in Chen Village.

Chen Xiaoxing walking his bicycle next
to an old Chenjiagou wall adorned
with depictions of Chen taiji postures.

A Master Teacher Emerges

As standard practice among the Chen Village boxers, Chen Xiaoxing started teaching at age 18. In 1976, he traveled throughout China teaching taiji. By the mid-1980's, his teaching ideas began to change. Based on direct influence from his brother, he began to focus more on teaching core taijiquan principles such as standing exercises (*zhan zhuang*) and silk-reeling. Chen Xiaoxing stated that because of this new approach, "by the 1990's, my teaching improved."

He now crafts his curriculum around the individual. He advises practitioners to focus on silk-reeling and standing exercises for their foundation. Chen Xiaoxing reminds us that, "The serious Chen taiji student should seek to achieve a balance of yin and yang forces in the body." He also advises that students follow Chen-style's traditional five stages of training (Chen, 1990: Section 4; Berwick, 1999: 189–195).

In the late 1990's, he took over the management of the village training center. The school is very much "community oriented" according to Daniel Poon, an Englishman who has been living in Chen Xiaoxing's home to study full-time at the village school. The school is a center of local exhibitions, often for large groups of visiting government officials or foreigners. When visitors are expected, the young students go into action cleaning the grounds and assembling seating and snacks for the audience. Under Chen Xiaoxing's supervision, great care and spirit go into these often last-minute performances.

Chen Xiaoxing says, "Taiji remains very popular in the village. The average Chen Village practitioner trains hard and possesses good skill. Most of the villagers are serious about taiji, but it is still hard to find protégés." Over the next few years, he hopes the school will offer regular academic subjects to the young live-in students, while remaining focused on taiji. He feels this will help attract and retain serious students.

Typical country hospitality belies his stature as the head boxing master in Chen Village. Very laid back and easy to talk to, Chen Xiaoxing treats foreign students as family guests. He remembers Chen-style starting to really become popular in 1979. He recalls, "In 1982, foreigners started to regularly visit the village, but in 1988, visits of foreigners decreased." Now he sees, "they are returning because China is becoming richer." He stated, "I invite all serious students—foreign and domestic—to come to Chen Village to train."

Students conversing on the footsteps
of the Chenjiagou Training Academy.

Training in Chen Village: The Foreign Student's Perspective

Short visits to Chen Village for specialized training have been the norm for a small, but increasing number of foreign enthusiasts. But committing to stay in the village for extended periods of training can be daunting for even the most hardy. One such foreigner, thirty-three year old U.K. born, Daniel Poon, embarked on this trek with a willingness and freedom to leave behind his normal comforts and diversions to train classically in an isolated, highly rural environment.

With only an intermediate conversational skill in Mandarin, Poon took advantage of Chen Xiaoxing's offer to teach all those of good character and high commitment. He has been living at Chen Xiaoxing's home for almost a year studying boxing full-time. A taiji practitioner since 1995, Poon is a student of the UK's Michael Tse. Poon stated that he "came to Chen Village with an excellent foundation in Chen-style from Tse," a well-regarded qigong instructor who also teaches Chen taijiquan. Poon came to the village with training in the old frame form of Chen-style and experience with the application practice of sparring and push-hands. At Chen Village, he learned new frame, weapons, and continues his training in push-hands. His experience and observations reveal the unique pleasures and peculiarities of training in today's Chen Village—as both a village resident and a foreigner.

Above: Students entering the Chenjiagou
Training Academy. Below: Training courtyard
in front of the Chenjiagou Training Academy
where people can be found practicing anytime.

At first, Poon studied under Chen Xiaoxing. He partly joked how "Chen
Xiaoxing didn't want me to get trounced on by the locals [in training]. When
you first get here, it can be overwhelming, so you need someone to hold your
hand." After training with Chen Xiaoxing, Poon began to train at the village
school. His learning then became "like osmosis." He describes the daily training
as "very informal." Poon advises that, "One can learn forms easily from many
in the village, but posture corrections are best had from the best instructors
here." He says that in the village, "although there are many who practice, the
best are the smartest ones."

Old Chen taiji lineage stone stile in the
foyer of the Chenjiagou Training Academy.

Youth sparring or "pushing" class in
the Chenjiagou Training Academy.

In Chen Village, training remains highly traditional, yet accessible. This may very well be Chen Village's greatest gift to the contemporary taiji student seeking classical training. While training in Chen Village is arduous, it is not as rigid and fast-paced as the large government-sponsored wushu academies that exist in China's major cities. Coeducational training is standard, except for the push-hands training. Training at the village academy is intense before some national competitions and the recently established biannual international competition held in Wen County, but is generally self-paced and progressive. Twice-per-day training sessions are the norm. Virtually all taiji students practice open-hand forms, weapons, and sparring daily. Poon observes, "Because of the physical hardship of the life here, along with the very young average starting age, training starts at a higher level. In the West, corrections are necessary for just learning how to stand properly, while in Chen Village posture corrections usually begin with the Single Whip posture."

From the beginning of training, the foundational old frame first form is emphasized without learning other material for long periods. In fact, the emphasis on perfecting the old frame first form continues for years, well into the advanced stages of proficiency that usually includes the new frame, weapons, and push-hands, plus plenty of wrestling and joint locking [qinna].

As a member of the village school, Poon is expected to participate in the demonstrations that occur frequently. Now considered a part of the Chen Village community, Poon insists, "I understand taiji's history and evolution much better." Unmistakably, his experience in Chen Village was, in essence, a step back in time, so as to move forward with his taijiquan.

* Translation assistance by Chen Pengfei and Ren Guangyi.

Bibliography

Berwick, S. (1997, October). Chen taijiquan combat training. *Inside Kung Fu*, 24(10), 189–195.

Chen, X. (1933). *Illustrated explanation of Chen family taijiquan*. No publisher given.

Chen, X. (1990). *Chen family transmission* (Chinese). Beijing: People's Sports Press.

Little, J. & Wong, C. (Eds.) (1999). *Ultimate tai chi*. Chicago: Contemporary Books.

Rich, H. (2000). Chen Style Taijiquan homepage. http://www.digidao. com.

Wallace, A. (1998). Internal training: The foundation for Chen taiji's fighting skills and health promotion. *Journal of Asian Martial Arts*, 7(1), 58–89.

Wile, D. (1996). *Lost tai chi classics from the late Ch'ing dynasty*. Albany, NY: State University of New York Press.

Chen Xiaowang on Learning, Practicing, and Teaching Chen Taiji

by Stephan Berwick

Chen Xiaowang demonstrating the
laojia version of Lazily Tying Coat.

The following is the only substantive interview Grandmaster Chen Xiaowang gave during his 2000 United States seminar tour. This is the first time Grandmaster Chen has shared the details of his early training and family history while offering profound insights into the practice and teaching of Chen taiji.

ON HISTORY

■ **What is your earliest martial arts memory?**
I remember waiting for my father, Chen Zhaoxu, to finish his morning practice before the family breakfast. Watching my father was like watching a movie. This gave me a sense or vision of what high-level taiji is. I didn't study his movements, I just watched him like a movie and retained the vision of what I saw.

■ **When did you begin training in taijiquan and what did you learn first? How serious was your training?**
I started training at the age of eight under my father. I practiced the old frame first form.

At thirteen, when I performed with a group of adult students, I caught the attention of the then senior village master teacher, Chen Zhaopei. When Chen Zhaopei saw me for the first time, he asked: "Whose kid is this?" So I was very serious with my taiji—even at that young age.

■ **What and when exactly did you study specific aspects of the art?**
I focused on the old frame until 1964, when my uncle, Chen Zhaokui, returned to Chen Village after staying with his father—the famous Chen Fake, who was my paternal grandfather—in Beijing. I was 18 then and began studying Chen Fake's new frame along with qinna. From 1972, I began to focus on the new frame. From 1974 to 1984, I really emphasized new frame and the strength-building training with the [sixteen-posture] Chen-style "big pole" [heavy long staff] form.

■ **When did you first compete?**
I first competed nationally in 1979. I later competed at the first ever international martial arts competition held in Xi'an [Shaanxi Province] in 1985. I've been fortunate to win gold medals consistently during my competition days.

■ **You were a senior martial arts official in the Chinese Government. How did this happen?**
I represented Henan Province at China's 1986 National Congress. Because of my fame and reputation, I was elected to an important senior-level post as head of martial arts for the huge Henan Province—a region full of important martial arts history, including the founding of taiji in my birthplace, Chen Village, and the home of the Shaolin Temple.

■ **When did you first begin your active international teaching career?**
From 1981 to 1985, I was routinely invited overseas, but the Chinese Government was concerned that a martial artist of my standing would leave and not return. But by 1985, many foreigners were visiting Chen Village to learn taiji. So finally in 1985, I was allowed to visit Japan for a few weeks to teach.

ON TEACHING

■ **How do you approach teaching today—especially in light of your experiences teaching Westerners with the popular seminar format?**
I believe everybody can be good at taiji. So I try to get students to understand taiji better. It is important to understand everybody—all people. I try to offer something individualized as much as possible. To best accomplish this with large groups, I approach each teaching session with a plan. I must be in an environment where I can control the room. Like a general, I speak very clearly while seeing and controlling the class. I never have a problem with the physical room in which a seminar is conducted. When I control the room, I control the students' minds.

■ **Your seminars routinely attract enthusiasts of diverse skill levels. How do you offer something for all, regardless of the material taught?**

There are three languages I use when teaching. They are the language of principles, the language of the body, and the language of corrections. I use different languages for different student levels. So there is no need for me to separate students based on their skill levels. My seminars are like buffet dinners: I offer different choices of courses, or languages, for different palates on one table.

■ **But are there any real differences when teaching the beginner versus the advanced student?**

When a student is a beginner, I follow him. As he improves, he then follows me.

ON TRAINING

■ **How should the modern Chen taiji boxer train?**

The traditional curriculum is still the preferred route to foundational training, which can take years to perfect. First you focus on old frame first form. Later, weapons, push-hands, and qinna are added.

■ **What about practicing the seemingly more popular new frame?**

The new frame is more detailed and difficult than the traditional old frame. It features more issuing energy (*fajing*). So before practicing the new frame, I recommend the traditional plan of training, of which the old frame is the core. The traditional plan is like first learning to drive. You have no control of the car. As you progress, you will gain more control of the vehicle—in this case, your body and mind—so that you can do more with the car.

■ **What are the most important qualities you recommend to students seeking to gain greater mind/body control?**

You must emphasize an understanding of qi flowing or qi direction. When you understand the meaning of qi flow, you will not have to rely on much physical power. Chen taiji students must remember the movement principles, such as the spiraling characteristic of silk-reeling energy. And always remember, the body follows the *dantian* (center).

■ **Can you elaborate on "following the dantian"?**

There are three basic principles: First when the dantian turns right, it also turns left. Second, when the dantian goes back, it also goes front. And third, principles one and two combine. My ancestor Chen Xin's important book on Chen taiji discusses these principles in great detail.

■ **What about the much sought after fali or fajing skills?**

Fali [issuing power] should occur naturally. It all goes back to applying the concepts to correct movement.

Chen Xiaowang demonstrating Parting the Horse's Mane (left)
and stepping at a recent seminar in New York City.

ON LEARNING

■ **What is your personal training like today?**

I remain focused on the details. Details are the most important things for me when seeking a higher level. Even though I teach so much now, I was never interested in making a living at this. I was always just concerned with the details.

■ **How are you still learning and improving?**

Even very recently there were some techniques that I only had a 50% understanding. For instance, in a 1997 seminar in Switzerland, a student tried to test my technique by suddenly and forcefully choking my neck from behind. I responded intuitively with fajing, using the rear elbow strike from the hidden hand punch technique, which hit him in his exposed xiphoid process. I was terrified to see that he immediately fell into cardiac arrest. To my relief, paramedics arrived in time to stabilize him. It was only after the incident that I fully understood that particular technique, because I never had to really use it before.

■ **What a story!**

I have many more. I love to tell stories, because I am still very much in love with taijiquan.

Dripping Oil Onto Parchment: Traditional Taijiquan Form Training in Chen Village

by David Gaffney, B.A.

Top: Familiarity through repetition.
Middle: Group demonstration in the main training hall in Chen Village.
Bottom: From an early age form training is used to develop strong foundation skills. Children in Wenxian County (close to Chen Village) practice the old frame form during a physical education class.
All photos courtesy of David Gaffney.

Introduction

Practicing taijiquan (often abbreviated as taiji) in its ancestral birthplace, Chen Village, allows one to cut through many misconceptions and to reach closer to the essence of the traditional manner of acquiring skill. The realization that you are tracing the footsteps of people like Chen Wangting (1600–1680), the creator of Chen taijiquan; Chen Changxing (1771–1853), formulator of the system as we know it today; and Chen Fake, who took taiji to the wider world, in effect, stepping on the same soil—gives one a great sense of continuity.

One area where East and West fully accord is in their belief that one should have a sense of the past to fully appreciate the present. That is why history is taught as a subject in school, and those of us who have been bored by it, and slept through the subject, are the poorer for it. With regards to taiji, perhaps even more important than recorded history is the method of acquiring skill that has been passed down orally from teacher to student for centuries.

Chen taiji has its own step-by-step comprehensive training method, of which, it soon becomes apparent, form training provides the foundation. Stories are handed down of the prodigious number of repetitions Chen Fake performed every day. Chen Xiaowang is said to have suspended building work on his house because it was interfering with his daily routine of thirty repetitions of the old frame first routine (*laojia yilu*). This tradition has survived with the current emerging masters from the village. Wang Haijun, three times overall champion in the Chinese National Taijiquan Tournament, recalled how his first eight years of training in Chen Village consisted solely of practicing the old frame first routine.

Form training is demanding. It requires the total attention and participation of mind and body. Elements such as patience, persistence, mind/intent (*yi*), strength, relaxation, and internal energy (*yi*) are crucial in honing one's taijiquan skills. In Chen Village, practitioners have for generations considered the hand form to be the base upon which all other taiji skills are built. Practicing the taiji form is not simply a matter of mindlessly repeating the sequences. Each routine has been carefully researched and meticulously arranged. The forms are the culmination of centuries of practical experience, each posture and maneuver having been tried, tested, and then assembled to construct the forms or routines we see today.

Characteristics of the Traditional Hand Forms

While modern shortened versions of taiji are practiced as an introduction to the system, the main curriculum emphasizes two primary bare-hand routines. The first and more commonly practiced routine is the first routine (*yilu*), the second being the more dynamic Cannon Fist routine (*Paochui*). The 14th-generation standard bearer Chen Changxing compiled these two routines, incorporating the more numerous ancient forms devised by systems founder Chen Wangting (Chen, 1993).

Chen Xiaowang performing the new frame (*xinjia*) routine.

Compared to the Cannon Fist, the first routine's movements are comparatively simple, with more emphasis placed upon softness than hardness. The first routine focuses upon the development of silk-reeling (*chansijing*) through the twining and coiling movements of the limbs and body, interspersed with issuing energy movements (*fajing*). In appearance, the form is relaxed, steady, and stable. The form, as the Chinese classics say, is "like a great river rolling on unceasingly." Throughout, the limbs are guided by the body in an uninterrupted sequence of opening and closing movements.

Great thought was given to the movements' features (hard or soft, difficult or easy, etc.) so that the art's complexities could be learned little by little over time. For instance, the first routine's beginning movements are relatively straightforward. The movements are comfortable and natural, with silk-reeling as the most important principle. More softness and less hard movement make learning and practicing easier. This employment of coiling and twining movement is one of the major features of Chen taiji. Practicing the form while accurately following this method leads the student along the path to developing more effective issuing energy, and, eventually gaining an understanding of how to apply and escape from joint-locking techniques (*qinna*). Conscientious training of the first form lays a strong base upon which more complex skills can subsequently be overlaid.

The second routine, Cannon Fist (*Paochui*), is more difficult. Movements are more intricate, faster, and tighter, with shaking energy as the main principle. Through practice of this form comes an appreciation of the different requirements of each movement—for example, the positioning of hands and feet, bodily synchronization throughout the movement, and how to place the body most favorably for attack or defense.

High or Low Postures?

The optimum number of forms practiced and the level of physical difficulty must be decided relative to the practitioner's strength, age, and vigor. For less-experienced students, it is preferable that actions be large, comfortable, and open. The expression of roundness, fullness, and continuous motion, as well as the alternation of opening and closing movements, can be more clearly seen when the spiraling silk-reeling circles are larger.

Practicing in a high or low stance is left up to personal preference. In the early stages of training, low postures allow one to develop the lower body's foundation strength. In a lecture entitled "How To Practice Taijiquan" given during the First International Chen Style Training Camp in 1999, Chen Zhenglei stressed the vital importance of building up leg strength. He suggested that:

> When the legs are strong and can bear weight firmly, then the upper body can relax and sink down into them, making the top flexible. If the legs are not strong, the upper body is "afraid" of sinking down and remains top heavy and unrelaxed.

Low postures also allow the practitioner to see more clearly the folding movements of the waist and turning of the legs. As the skill level increases, it is normal for the postures to become higher. This higher stance is extremely agile, the practitioner being able to change naturally and easily between high and low positions. For the older beginner, a higher position may be more comfortable. Above all, in practicing the form, one should let naturalness be the guiding principle.

Training the Frame (Lien Panjia)

The inhabitants of Chen Village refer to taiji practice as "training the frame of one's posture" (*lien panjia*). Great emphasis is placed on the quality of a student's position and fixing any deficiencies in his or her posture. The training syllabus requires the student to first learn the form's movements. Once familiarity with the form is reached, the process of correcting posture can begin. Correcting posture is a "hands on" process whereby the teacher adjusts the posture of a student until it eventually fulfills a set of requirements handed down over many generations. This is achieved in much the same way as a sculptor refining ever-greater details from a crude outline.

Correcting posture is
a hands-on process.
Chen Xiaowang
helping Mr. Gaffney.

Familiarity Through Repetition

Chen Zhenglei likens the process of achieving competence in the form to learning to write Chinese characters. In the early stages of practice one should not look too far ahead to the more advanced requirements. Like learning the basic calligraphy strokes, the beginner should first concern himself with accurately learning the sequence. Concentration should be focused upon maintaining an upright position and performing the movements in a soft and balanced manner. Inexperienced practitioners often try to run before they can walk and would do well to heed the following advice:

> As for those errors that unavoidably crop up—like raising your shoulders or sticking out your elbows, filling your chest with unrestrained qi, panting when you breathe, your hands and feet trembling, etc.—it is not advisable to delve into these phenomena too deeply. – Chen, 1998

Different teachers from Chen Village often compare learning taijiquan to the wider educational system. Everybody accepts that they must go through primary education before they are ready to attend high school. Likewise, they must complete high school before they can attend a university. Those trying to acquire the more complex skills upon an inadequate foundation are destined to fail.

Repetitive practice of the form leads to familiarity with the movements. Certain optimum patterns of movement must be established, and these can only become set if they are repeated almost endlessly. Chen Zhenglei (1999) said that taijiquan movement's unique nature is designed to get rid of all body stiffness and rigidity. Through prolonged practice and training, the body's joints are loosened, the tendons are stretched and elongated, and all parts of the body are coordinated in motion. Every gap between the joints should eventually develop an elastic quality. This elasticity—the stretching of the tendons, plus developing whole body coordination—is what is known as taiji internal skill (*neigong*) (Si, 2000: 13).

The tomb of
Chen Zhoukui.

In time, coordination, flexibility, and relaxation are acquired throughout every movement within the form. The movement becomes fluid and unpredictable, changing instantly form slow to fast, from soft to hard, and from light to heavy. Relaxation provides the foundation of accumulating and releasing power (*fajing*). By seeking complete relaxation, the practitioner attempts to rid himself of stiff energy released *en route* during a movement. Speed and power is greatly increased by lessening the stiff resistance of muscles during movement (Si, 2000: 13).

In his discourse on fighting methods, *Training for Sparring*, Chen Zhaokui writes:

> Emphasis on slow movements alone leads to slow strikes which an opponent can counter easily. Emphasis on fast moves only makes it difficult to feel the path of your energy and makes it easy to strike along a longer path than necessary. Being fast refers to the speed generated through familiarity of the energy path. It is a speed without loss of quality.
>
> – Ma, 1998

Slowness as a Training Tool

When training the form, emphasis is placed upon slowness. Throughout each individual movement, the practitioner begins slowly, moves smoothly in transition, and gradually settles into the final posture. Using the slow approach allows one to fully concentrate upon each opening and closing, stretch and withdraw, and rising and lowering movement. Over time, slow practice enables postures to be developed exactly, to fulfill the martial applications contained within. Every form trains the body so that the practitioner becomes aware of the optimum position through all stages of each technique, and slowness enables the body to become fixed in its postures. Following this approach, when a movement is speeded up, it becomes natural and will not stray. Posture and movement developed in this way will grow to be habitual and can be utilized whenever an individual needs to move quickly and decisively—whether they are speeding up the movements of the form, practicing push hands, or engaging in free-sparing (*san shou*).

Exponents of the external martial arts generally consider the development of direct force and superior speed and strength as the natural way by which an adversary can be defeated. From this perspective, taiji seems to be at odds with nature. At first glance, it seems obvious that, in combat, strength must be superior to softness and speed more successful than slowness. Taiji philosophy, however, holds that this assessment is invalid. Instead, taiji followers are asked to have confidence in the idea that softness can prevail over greater strength and that slowness can defeat speed. Performing movements quickly before the postures have become fixed and exact leads to a loss of detail and efficacy. Consequently, the use of slowness represents one of taiji's distinctive training methods rather than its ultimate objective.

Vital energy (qi), spirit (shen), intention (yi).
Calligraphy by Zhu Tiancai.

Fostering Mental Calmness and Its Roll Cultivating Qi, and the Development of Intention

Calmness of the mind is a fundamental requirement if the practitioner hopes to preserve the many finer points contained inside the forms. Impatience merely leads to hurriedness and a loss of detail. Composure of the mind enables vital energy to become quiet and subsequently to follow the intention. In this manner the intention can be fostered, facilitating the link between spirit (*shen*) and vital energy (*qi*). Chen Zhenglai (1998) suggests that:

> In practicing Chen-style taijiquan, you must keep your thoughts quiet, getting rid of all internal and external disturbances. Only in this way will you benefit by restraining your internal energy, and by guiding the rising up and movement of internal energy.

In time, this approach allows the taiji practitioner to effect whole-body movement during the form, unifying internal spirit or consciousness with the external form, thereby uniting body and mind. Practicing slowly allows one to cultivate qi, increasing the health and vigor of the body. This provides the foundation from which martial stamina and skill can flourish.

Traditional taiji practice emphasizes the importance of the abdominal center of balance (*dantian*) and its rotation. When form training, the practitioner is required to focus on the dantian region. According to the study of meridians, the dantian is situated in the lower abdomen two to three fingers below the navel. In this area, there is a concentration of internal organs, mainly the reproductive and excretory ones. Concentrating one's mind intent on the dantian has several benefits: 1) it can lower the body's center of gravity making the lower plane (*xia pan*) very steady and balanced, 2) it enables massage of the internal organs, which increases the functions of those organs, 3) it can focus the mind-intent (*yi nien*) so that when you are practicing boxing you are actually resting your mind, and 4) it enables dantian breathing, namely abdominal breathing, which increases lung capacity (Si, 2000: 13).

In order not to hinder qi development, the forms should be practiced according to the principles, and one should not place a limit on each movement by focusing on one particular application. Every movement has many possible applications. Considering each as part of a circle, one realizes that all points on the circle can represent a particular application, depending on the situation. One should learn the method, not its manifestation (Chen, 1999). In other words, do not be concerned with individual applications but rather on how the body moves as a completely integrated system.

Fundamental to correct taiji practice is the constant involvement of the mind (*yi*) in all movements within the form arising from the mind's "intent." The mind moves the qi, which in turn moves the body. The taiji form requires the practitioner to develop a deep level of concentration upon the body's internal sensations, at all times focusing on the precise movement being performed. In terms of strictness and attention to detail, even the smallest detail must be clearly executed, with no brushing over a movement that is unclear. Each movement within the sequence should be carefully considered as to its function and characteristics: whether it is relaxed enough, where to open and close, whether to turn in the foot, if there is enough spiral movement, etc. The practitioner meticulously works out the requirements, slowly reducing the number of shortcomings and faults. With this mindset, each repetition of the form should lead to new discoveries and understandings, and ultimately mastery.

To develop *yi* and qi, the form must be practiced correctly for some time. Distinct stages must be passed through. First, the sequence must be mastered until it becomes very familiar. At this stage, emphasis is placed primarily upon attaining looseness in the joints and correct body structure. Initially, training should center on standardizing the movements of the form as closely as possible to fulfill the body requirements of Chen taijiquan. Each time the student comes to a fixed posture—for example, Lazily Tying Coat (*lan zha yi*), Single Whip (*dan bian*), or preparing form (*taiji qi shi*)—he or she should focus strictly upon each part of the body, making sure that it conforms to the principles. This process requires considerable mental effort if the student is to avoid deviating from the correct path. Though many people can quote the taiji requirements and verses from the taiji classics, real understanding can only come through training these into one's body. For instance, it is not enough to know that the shoulders must be relaxed; the practitioner must discover how to relax them and to what degree. Or how to contain or store the chest (*han xiong*). At what point is it sufficiently stored? Too much, and the waist collapses; too little, and the shoulder tightens.

Once the form can be performed naturally, the internal energy can develop. With each completed posture, the vital energy sinks to the dantian and from there is distributed throughout the body. Through continual, diligent practice, more qi is accumulated and stored in the dantian. Chen Zhenglai (1999) likens the dantian to a large river, saying that if the water level is not sufficiently high, then water will not fill the smaller tributaries downstream. So, if the dantian has not filled with qi, qi cannot be pushed out to the extremities.

When the fixed postures have been standardized and the basic requirements fulfilled, the practitioner then must consider the movement principles: using the waist as the axis, moving sectionally, etc. At this stage, one must seek the correct route of each movement in the form, incorporating the basic requirements and movement principles. To understand one or two points is considered not bad, as it is not possible to understand every aspect at once. Improvement occurs in a step-by-step manner over time. For example, dividing the body into three sections, a requirement of all basic movements is that the outer sections (hands and feet) hold the energy, the two middle sections (elbows and knees) hold the position, and the two root sections (shoulders and upper thighs, *ku*) relax. To do all of this simultaneously is very difficult, so it is better perhaps to concentrate on one point at a time (Si, 2000: 13). As the movement principles and body requirements are realized, the internal energy from the dantian can be accurately directed to the appropriate point, depending upon which movement is being performed.

The Hand Form as a Blueprint for Developing Martail Skill

The hand form provides the blueprint for developing the martial skills of Chen taijiquan. A multifaceted instructional tool, it incorporates many essentials that, when united, allow the practitioner to fully build up his fighting skills. There are no easy options if one seeks to acquire higher-level abilities. Inexperienced students often press the teacher as to the precise application and usage of particular movements early in their training. With the traditional Chen Village masters, answers sometimes seem ambiguous and vague. Instead of being shown some spectacular attack or countering technique, the student is told to look to the principle behind the movement. This can be very frustrating to those used to being spoon fed techniques, after all, it is argued, if you don't learn how to attack an opponent, how can this be a martial art? Impatient students may leave with the feeling that the real skill is being withheld or may gloomily conclude that their skill is not deemed sufficient to warrant an answer.

Chen Zhenglei in transition movement during the "lazily tying coat" posture.

During class one day, Chen Zhenglai likened taiji's martial application to Chinese medicine with its emphasis on cause rather than symptom. One should, he suggested, try to understand how a movement is generated rather than focusing upon its final expression. Approached in this manner, the form becomes a training method to ready the body for combat. In a treatise entitled "Training Method of Chen Taiji Routine and Push Hands," Chen Zhaokui writes: "every position should be precise and each destination should be clear" (Ma, 1998).

Taiji is a practical and no-nonsense martial art. Its proficient use rests upon an assimilation of its core principles if one is to grasp the internal substance and avoid the practice "flowery fists": nice to look at, but devoid of content. At all times, the practitioner must seek out the most difficult, the most challenging, and the most detailed aspects of the movements contained within the form. The temptation to cheat to circumvent demanding movements should be avoided. For instance, when performing the Dragon on the Ground posture, the practitioner drops into a low stance, and next, even more difficult, moves to the following position through arced movement.

Every movement and step in the form has been developed to prepare the student for a particular purpose, and all ought to be viewed as being important, not just those with immediately apparent martial applications.

Old Frame First Routine — Closing Sequence
1) crossed foot kick (*shi zhi jiao*)
2) punch to crotch (*zhi dang chui*)
3) white ape presents fruit (*bai yuan xian guo*)
4) six sealing and four closing (*liu feng si bi*)

5) single whip (*dan bian*)

6) dragon on the ground (*que di long*)

7) stepping forward with seven stars (*shang bu qi xing*)

8) step back to ride the tiger (*xia bu kua hu*)

9) head-on blow (*dang tou pao*)

10) Buddha's warrior attendant pounds mortar (*jin gang dao dui*)

11) closing form (*taiji shou si*)

Requirements When Practicing the Form

In his book *Chen Style Taijiquan Method and Theory*, Ma Hong (1998), a disciple of Chen Zhaokui, lists sixteen requirements laid down by his teacher, which must be attended to during each posture:

1) eye movement (the direction of the eyes)
2) the shape of the hands, and how the hand changes as the movement is being performed
3) silk-reeling (*shun-chan* and *ni-chan*) of the arms
4) footwork (how to execute changes when stepping)
5) silk-reeling (*shun-chan* and *ni-chan*) of the legs
6) opening and closing of the chest and back
7) rising and falling of the buttocks
8) dantian rotation (waist and lower abdomen)
9) shifting weight (the relationship of substantial and insubstantial)
10) beginning and end points, as well as the transitional movements of the upper and lower limbs
11) how much strength to use, and where the strength should be concentrated (i.e., where is the attack point?)
12) position and direction of posture
13) the rise and fall of spiral movement (top and bottom coordination)
14) the change in tempo (alternating slow and fast)
15) breathing (coordination of breathing and movement)
16) listening (not just auditory, but with all senses)

The requirements are not rigid measurements but have got to be experienced and polished through continuous training. Their intricacy is reflected in an early taiji adage: "Only the gods know; impossible to transmit orally." To the inexperienced learner, Chen taijiquan's body requirements at times appear almost unbearably strict. Nevertheless, by following this route, an advanced level of ability can be reached in a step-by-step manner.

Over time, conscientious practice and study of the form allow the practitioner to identify and build into his arsenal both the attacking and defensive facets of the art. From a defensive perspective, the intention is to achieve the capacity to lure an adversary into emptiness. This requires training to a stage where one can stick, connect, adhere, and follow; neither losing contact with nor resisting the opponent. Offensive skills are acquired by refining taiji's eight energy methods (*ba fa*): *peng, lu, ji, an, cai, lei, zhou, and kou.* In time, the student tries to approach the level of skill often quoted in the taiji classics whereby "four ounces can overcome a thousand pounds."

To attain this level, the form must be honed until it becomes unbroken, with each movement flowing smoothly into the next, on the surface relaxed but inwardly strong. Where hard and soft elements are combined, the upper and lower body are coordinated, and the internal and external (*yi* and *li*) work closely together. Looking at accomplished practitioners, you see movement that is highly refined, devoid of all stiffness and clumsiness.

The development pace cannot be forced. Paradoxically, the more you try to hurry, the more difficult it is to progress. Highly regarded 20th generation practitioner Wang Haijun, an adopted student of Chen Zhenglai, cites an old Chen taiji saying that skill is acquired like dripping oil onto parchment until eventually the parchment is saturated. He says that the traditional way was to accept whatever the teacher was teaching at whatever pace, no matter how slowly. With prolonged practice, skill naturally develops. Those people who train daily for years reach levels of skill that seem impossible to achieve to those unable or unwilling to devote themselves as fully to training.

While individual goals dictate the level of intensity during practice, combat efficiency necessitates a high level of dedication in terms of time and exertion. The forms should not be approached as sequences of movements and techniques to be memorized and then repeated parrot-like. Rather, they are training tools with which one can hone the ability to move and react in a calm, natural, and potent way. Chen Xiaowang, in his critique "The Fajing of Chen Style Taijiquan" (n.d.), suggests that a fitting outlook when practicing the form is to train diligently, ignoring tiredness, and accepting the need to work hard. In the words of a well-known Chinese saying, if you hope to reach a high level of skill, you must be willing to "eat bitterness" (chi ku).

Bibliography

Chen, X. (n.d.). "The fajing of Chen Style Taijiquan," downloaded from Chen Zhenglei's official website: http://www.chenzhenglei-tj.com. In Chinese.

Chen, Z. (1993). Wonderful taiji kungfu. Zhengzhou: Zhengzhou Ancient Books.

Chen, Z. (1998). Chinese taijiquan scriptures: Taijiquan Chen shi jia dushu. Xi'an: Qu Ban Xian Gongsi.

Chen, Z. (1999). Notes taken during the First International Chen Taijiquan Training Camp, held in August 18th to the 28th in Handang, Hebei, China.

Ma, H. (1998). Chen Style Taijiquan method and theory. Beijing: Beijing Sports University Press.

Si, C. (2000). Demystifying taijiquan, Shaolin and Taiji, 11: 13. In Chinese.

An Encounter with Chen Xiaowang: The Continuing Development of Chen-Style Taijiquan

by Dietmar Stubenbaum

Photographs courtesy of Chen Xiaowang.

Introduction

The following material is provided as a result of a visit made to Chen Xiao-wang's house in Australia in November, 1993. I stayed in his home for one week in order to receive personal instruction in Chen-style taijiquan and also to arrange this interview. One of the first things I noticed about Chen Xiaowang is his extremely busy schedule. He is kept busy teaching, giving many private lessons and also instructing various groups. In most of his classes, students are learning the new Chen-style form he created which contains thirty-eight movements. In other classes students are studying the first and second routines of the old family (laojia) system, and some advanced students are studying the "sticky spear."

I studied every day with him for about three hours. When could we conduct an interview? It was difficult to find time because he was either busy teaching, interpreters were not available, or there was some such distraction. Luckily, we finally did find time to sit down to talk. Two of Mr. Chen's students, Ms. Pow Yin Chau and Mr. Francis Heng, assisted in interpreting. Without their kind help the interview would have been impossible. But even with their help, it was difficult to conduct an indepth interview as I would have liked. For example, questions regarding lineage could not be answered satisfactorily since some resource materials which could have provided answers were still in China. Also, there was a collection of photographs in China which could have been used to illustrate the history and evolution of Chen taijiquan. So, in addition to the interview, I present some information regarding the instruction I received personally as well as the general impression I received of this nineteenth-generation Chen-style taijiquan master.

Chen Xiaowang and Dietmar Stubenbaum
at the airport in Australia.

Chen Xiaowang—The Gentleman

As a famous Chinese "cultural treasure," it is surprising to find how friendly Chen Xiaowang can be. Unlike many other martial art masters who choose to remain aloof, Mr. Chen is quite personable. Perhaps it was because his wife and three sons are not yet in Australia that he welcomed my company. Or perhaps part of his openness came from knowing my own interest in Chen-style taijiquan as an adopted "Chen family" member in the lineage of Tu Zongren and Du Yuze, which stemmed from his great grandfather Chen Yanxi. Or perhaps his kindness came simply from his being a gentleman who enjoys being hospitable to guests. When he told me, "Make yourself at home," it was easy to see that he meant it. One of the pleasures this invitation offered was the opportunity to watch hours of his video collection, which proved highly instructional in itself.

Mr. Chen is a quiet person who feels very comfortable here in his peaceful home in Australia. He's a very simple man who likes to relax in between his hectic schedule. When home, he often goes outside to eat fruit, to float in his pool on an inflated raft, or to converse with friends. A big flower garden perfumes the area and draws an array of chirping birds.

Mr. Chen goes to sleep early since he gets up quite early every morning to exercise. Sometimes he goes through the taijiquan forms, but he also spends much time on qigong practice. Nearing fifty years of age, Mr. Chen looks very healthy and much younger than he is. He has a very strong build, especially his legs. Without being muscle-bound, his upper body has very smooth features. He is strong and powerful, continually maintaining a very straight posture in his taijiquan and daily movements.

People from around the world have contacted Mr. Chen for lessons in taijiquan. Many of his students studied from other teachers of various styles. Their past martial art experience helps them to realize how lucky they are now to be studying with Mr. Chen. Much of his personality can be seen in how he teaches. He teaches in his own way. The best way to describe this is to write about my own experience studying with him. Looking back over my years of martial art training in Europe, Japan and Taiwan, this experience proved to be the most insightful.

Chen Xiaowang's three-year-old son performing
Buddha's Warrior Attendant Pounds Mortar.

Method of Instructing

As mentioned previously, I studied with Chen Xiaowang for three hours per day for one week. Although I already learned the two routines of laojia in Taiwan from Mr. Tu Zongren, Mr. Chen chose to teach me a basic qigong practice to start. This was a standing qigong practice in which one stands erect with both hands extended to the front at chest level, palms facing each other.

Even in this simple posture, Mr. Chen's corrections seemed to offer an endless stream of advice on how to make improvements. The overriding advice was to relax: relax the arms, relax the breathing, relax the legs, feet, little toe. Relax, relax, relax. . . . This basic exercise focuses on letting the qi flow into the hands and to other areas of the body. One ends the exercise by lowering the hands to the dantian, the area a few inches below the navel, and rotating the hands thirty-six times to the left and then to the right.

After I had done this qigong practice for a few days, following all of Mr. Chen's detailed corrections, for the first time ever I felt a very strong feeling of qi moving in my body. Some real changes occurred which I would not have experienced without Mr. Chen's guidance. I felt extremely comfortable even with these basic exercises. I think the primary reason for any progress made was his ability to direct my practice into a deeper state of relaxation than I could have reached before.

Mr. Chen then proceeded to give instruction in individual taijiquan movements, paying attention to movements focusing on single-hand movements, double-hand movements, and the basic steps. Just by visual observation, he can identify any place where one's muscles are tight and where they are relaxed. He points out exactly how the hands and elbows have to be, how and why the qi flows or stops. At the same time, he often explains qi movement by referring to acupuncture points. He may show how the qi circulates from the small finger to the shoulder or how it moves from the hands to the back at the same level as the dantian, through reference to the meridians found in acupuncture charts. He teaches these basics in such a detailed fashion that through practice it becomes easier to visualize the internal movement of qi. The results can be felt in better concentration and in the awareness of changes occurring in the body regarding the qi flow.

We then incorporated these lessons in correcting my practice of the first of the two routines of the laojia system. The rest of my lessons focused on improving this routine. Even though I had been practicing this set for years, in a short time the set felt much more comfortable under Mr. Chen's guidance. He also showed me some of the standard applications for each technique in the set, including Single Whip, Buddha's Warrior Attendant Pounds Pestle, etc. He used numerous holding techniques (qinna) on me. This proved to be an extremely painful experience! Whenever I tried to attack or push him in any way, I quickly found that I just couldn't do anything. At the same time, his techniques flowed easily according to his will. Previous to this, I thought I had some knowledge about how to push someone. With him, it was just like trying to push a void. I just couldn't move him no matter how I tried. It was impossible. If one were to try to push him, one would be thrown several meters. In fact, I fell down quite often following my attempts to topple him. These practical lessons left no doubt about how fully he knows his art.

Mr. Chen is very, very powerful and knows the martial applications to perfection. I have never seen anyone playing taijiquan as well as he, plus his method of instruction is clear and easy to understand. He gives the student all the information he needs to make very fast progress. Of course, Mr. Chen has his price for his instruction, which I found to be worth the investment.

Mr. Chen practices four standard routines of the taijiquan system: laojia, first and second routines, and xinjia, two routines developed by Chen Fake. In addition he has developed his own Thirty-Eight Style routine. Two-person practices include push-hands and the sticky-spear routines. He also trains with all weapons, including the single-sword, double-swords, single-dao, double-dao, spear, and halberd. Mr. Chen masterfully performs the competition Yang form and other taijiquan forms. He must know these well since he serves as a judge in many of the taijiquan competitions. His focus, however, remains on the Chen system.

Chen Xiaowang corrects a student's form
during a seminar in Italy. On the right,
he is illustrating an application of
Buddha's Warrior Attendant Pounds Mortar.

Some Specific Questions
Answered by Chen Xiaowang

■ **What responsibilities do you have as the nineteenth-generation representative of Chen taijiquan?**
Simply to pass on taijiquan traditions to the next generation, so all can appreciate it; to preserve the principles of taijiquan; bring taijiquan up-to-date so people today can accept and appreciate it. Maintain the traditional theories, but be able to pass it on; to adapt it to modern situations because people have different requirements today.

■ **Regarding your method of instruction, do you consider yourself a traditionalist?**

I maintain the old traditional methods of teaching, such as the teaching from father-to-son which is a one-to-one concept. I also started teaching in a modern way, adapting to the different cultures, different religions, different people. I can't just show the movements. Taijiquan is not just the feeling of hands; it is the actual feeling of the particular person. In order to understand and appreciate the details of taijiquan, I must modify everything to fit different cultural backgrounds, trying to fit my teaching to the psychological makeup of people. In this way I see taijiquan progressing as part of world culture.

It is something I value passing on and will not change it, but I must transfer it through the language and culture of my students so they can fully understand all the aspects of taijiquan.

■ **Is there any connections between Cheng Style taijiquan and the Shaolin Temple?**
No influence.

■ **Besides the name being derived from Daoism, is there any special religious or philosophical practices which were or still are observed in Chen taijiquan?**
Daoism, yin-yang, five-element theories . . . No doubt about the influence of Daoist principles in the practice of taijiquan. These principles are the very foundation of taijiquan.

■ **Are medical aspects part of the study of taijiquan?**
No matter what walk of life, no matter what race or nationality you are—German, French, Chinese . . . differences in height, complexion or whatever—the only thing in common among us is yin-yang and the presence of qi. In this respect, we are all the same. Taijiquan differs from traditional Chinese medicine, but it works on the same principles, e.g., open-close, qi moving up and down. So, the only thing in common among us is the presence of qi. If the qi is balanced, then you are healthy. Therefore, all can study taijiquan. Since Chinese medical practices are based on the yin-yang concept, so taijiquan is part of this system.

■ **Have the routines changed much over the years?**
There have definitely been some minor changes, but the movements are all the same.

■ **If you want to learn the whole system, what do you have to practice?**
Taijiquan is part of our life style and forms a vital part of our daily activity. So, by principle, we traditionally start with the first routine of laojia; afterwards one can proceed to the second level. But this depends on the time we can devote to practice. After one learns the standing qigong, the Thirty-Eight Style, and the first routine and all the basic principles are understood, then it is possible to proceed to the second routine (Paochui). Xinjia, arranged by Chen

Fake, is also included. And now we practice four routines based on the old and new styles.

■ **Who are the main teachers in the Chen Village today?**
There are many very capable teachers. Actually quite a few.

■ **From Chen-style taijiquan came the Yang-style. Has the Yang-style influenced the Chen-style in anyway?**
No.

■ **The teachings in Chen Village were secret. Has this changed?**
There are no secrets anymore.

■ **Since there are no secrets, the main obstacle in perfecting one's taijiquan is the limitation of time. How can we make the best of our practice?**
To get the real benefits of Chen taijiquan, even to practice only one form is enough for the health purposes. Studying the Thirty-Eight Style is enough. You can understand how the qi flows and other aspects of the art. But to study the whole Chen system, you need to study seriously for a very long time. I can teach the whole system, but students must study step-by-step; otherwise they cannot understand the higher levels of practice. One must progress by levels. If you have not mastered the basics, naturally the most advanced levels cannot be taught. If you can appreciate and absorb each level of Chen taijiquan practice and have the time to devote to continue regular practice, then the whole system can be learned.

■ **Should one focus on practicing taijiquan movements or on qi flow?**
If your movement is not correct, your qi will not flow. . . . Every time you move—if you are practicing the routines, push-hands, weapons—every movement, if it is not correct, the movement will be empty. As a result, your form would be purely physical. There will be no qi inside. This is a very important point. It doesn't matter what style you practice. If you practice in the wrong way, you cannot get the full benefit out of martial arts practice. This is why many practice very often but cannot get the full benefit from their work. However, if you are able to master the basics, doing what lets the qi flow, this is the most important point. If you can understand this, then all else is easier to learn.

■ **Who were your teachers?**
My father Chen Zhaoxu, my father's cousin Chen Zhaopi and my father's younger brother Chen Zhaokui.

■ **We have not read much about your father, Chen Zhaoxu. Can you tell us a little about him and his involvement in taijiquan?**
My father, Chen Zhaoxu, had knowledge in all aspects of taijiquan that went

very deep. Even at twenty-two years of age his skills were so high that many boxing masters came to Beijing to see him. This left him satisfied with his youthful talent to the point that he didn't even practice much. But this attitude soon changed. One day a visitor came to see my father. This visitor was also a highly skilled martial artist. In seeking to test the visitor's skill, my father tried to push him from behind. His attempt not only failed to budge the visitor, but my father ended up tossed to the ground. This experience humiliated my father, who returned to his room, closed the doors and didn't talk with anyone. He practiced secluded for three days. My grandfather, Chen Fake, was also very embarrassed by this incident. He tested my father by repeating the same techniques used when the visitor proved himself superior in the confrontation. My father, with renewed dedication to the art, continued to practice with my grandfather and reached a higher level in taijiquan skills.

Not much later another boxing expert, about the same age as my father, came to visit. The visitor had great boxing skills, but when he tried to attack, my father defended himself quickly and effectively by uprooting the boxer, sending him as high as the house rafters. This was nearly three meters high. My father caught him before he hit the floor so the visitor would not be hurt from the fall.

News of this incident spread quickly. Many heard the rumors of my father's skills and he continued to have visitors that came to test his skills. His movements became so spontaneous and natural that no one could throw him to the floor again!

Chen Xiaowang is also well known for his calligraphy. The character
above means "to dance" or "to brandish." Below: Chen Xiaowang,
ninteenth-generation representative of Chen family style, demonstrates
some of the taijiquan movements which were passed down through his family.
Photos courtesy of Chen Xiaowang.

FACTS ABOUT CHEN XIAOWANG

- Date of birth: October 20, 1946.
- Place of birth: Chen Village, Henan Province, People's Republic of China.
- Awards: Taijiquan gold medalist at three consecutive National Wushu Tournaments in 1980, 1981 and 1982. Taijiquan champion at the first International Wushu Competition held at Xi'an, China in 1985.
- Positions held: Taijiquan instructor in China (1980 to 1987).
  Senior Wushu instructor (equivalent to a university associate professor) in China (1988 to present).
  Chairperson of the Henan Province Chen Style Taijiquan Association.
  Technical advisor and official assessor for the standardized competition routine for the Chen, Yang, Wu and Sun taijiquan styles.
- Appointed by the Chinese National Sports Committee in 1985 to draft rules and regulations for taijiquan competitions both domestically and internationally.
- President of the Cultural Exchange Association of Henan Province.
- President of the Society of Chinese Calligraphy and Literature.
- Author: *Chen Style Taijiquan* (1985) and *Chen Style Taijiquan 38 Form* (1984) published by the Sports Publications Centre of the People's Republic of China.

Going Beyond the Norm: An Interview with Chen Taijiquan Stylist Wang Xi'an

by Asr Cordes*

Chen-style Grandmaster Wang Xi'an.
All photographs courtesy of A. Cordes and Cheng Jincai.

Introduction

Wang Xi'an, a nineteenth-generation Chen-style taijiquan practitioner, is one of the leading representatives of the style. He is one of the celebrated Chen-style "Four Great Tigers," the others being Chen Xiaowang, Chen Zhenglei, and Zhu Tiancai. Mr. Wang has played a unique role in the preservation and proliferation of Chen taiji in Chen Village (*Chenjiagou*), where the style originated, and around the world.

Wang was born in 1944 in Xi'an, Shanxi Province, China. He and his family moved to Chen Village in 1945; Wang's parents were natives of Chen Village. About 120 years ago, Wang family ancestors moved to Chen Village from Xingyang Village, which is south of the Yellow River.

Like most Chen villagers, Wang Xi'an began learning taiji when he was very young. However, his formal training did not begin until an eighteenth-generation successor of the style, Chen Zhaopei, retired from his civil service job and returned to Chen Village in 1958. He found that the level of taiji had diminished to the point that the standards of the next generation were uncertain.

He subsequently opened up the first formal classes. It was in these classes that Wang Xi'an and the other "Four Great Tigers" were taught. The "Four Great Tigers" subsequently studied with eighteenth-generation masters Chen Zhaokui and Feng Zhiqiang.

Wang Xi'an draws on his lifetime of Chen-style training to clearly communicate the mindset of Chen practice as well as vital keys to achieving success in Chen taijiquan training.

In May 2000, Wang made his first visit to the United States. In an effort to improve taiji here, two of Wang's students, Cheng Jincai (a lineage disciple and thirty-year student of Wang) and Li Shudong, sponsored Wang's visit. The following interview was conducted in Chinese Mandarin at Cheng Jincai's Chen Style Tai Chi Development Center in Houston, Texas.

INTERVIEW

Asr Cordes, author and
Chen-style practitioner.

■ **How did you came to study taiji?**

Well, it was the tradition and specialty of the area. Prior to the Cultural Revolution [1966–1976], everyone living in the village practiced. It was almost as if you couldn't live there without doing it. As a child living there you see everyone doing it, so naturally you try it too.

When I began learning taiji, all of the people there were farmers. During the busy seasons, training was put on hold. When the farm work was done, training continued. At that time, taiji training was in the background of my life.

■ **At what point did you become serious about studying taiji?**

My serious training began when I was around eighteen years old, but my formal training didn't begin until I was twenty. At that time, Chen Zhaopei had returned to Chen Village and began teaching formal classes. Before Chen Zhaopei organized formal classes, everyone had their own small training groups and areas, usually at home. Family members of all different ages trained together. There were no big classes or anything like that.

I first studied small frame Chen-style and then large frame. I would like to note that the Chen small and large frames have a few difference between them. Based on my experience and observations, the old large frame of Chen-style yields a faster rate of development.

■ **We have heard that you have been instrumental in helping to preserve and promote Chen taiji. Could you tell us a little bit about that?**

Throughout the past, the popularity of taiji in Chen Village has had its ups and downs due to different events. The most recent down period was during the ten years of the Cultural Revolution. During the Cultural Revolution, I was in a unique position to help keep taiji going in the village as I held the position of *dui zhang*, which is like a vice mayor. Chen Zhaopei gave me the special responsibility of maintaining and promoting taiji development in the village. I knew I would need the help of the other teachers in the village. I invited Chen Zhaokui, an eighteenth-generation representative, back to the Chen Village to teach the new frame system of his father, Chen Fake.

I sought out the assistance of the local government leaders to help restore and promote the growth of taiji practice in and around the village. We organized all of the small training groups into formal town classes. We put in place compulsory regulations that made it mandatory that these small groups form town classes. If a person trained well, they would receive special awards such as pay bonuses. If a person trained poorly, there might be pay deductions or overtime hours issued. These different groups also had small competitions in which people would receive special awards.

I also brought taiji training into the elementary and middle school curriculum. In addition to this, I opened up school and public classes for advanced practitioners to bring them up to a higher level. After a few years, I opened up a professional training school [*ti xiao*] with middle- and advanced-level classes. As a result, everyone in the village was into taiji training.

The Japanese began to develop a strong interest in taijiquan in 1981. After studying Yang Taiji for a year, they learned that the major taiji styles had developed from Chen taiji and that the Chen Village was the source of taiji. In 1982, they approached the Henan Province Sports Committee about learning taiji in the Chen Village. I went as a representative to meet and interview the Japanese. In 1982, they brought a group of taiji enthusiasts from Japan to study at Chen Village. This was the first time the village had been opened up to other countries.

This event drew such a large crowd that many police were needed to provide security. The event received lots of publicity from both the local and Japanese media. A well-known Japanese journalist, Shan Po Yinfu [Mandarin], was among this first group of visitors. He invited me to visit Japan in 1983. Japanese television and newspapers covered this visit extensively. I set up coaches for many cities in Japan and returned to China. About this time, taiji in general started to gain more popularity around the world.

Later, the Henan Sports Committee wanted me to go and teach in other areas. A few years later the other members of the "Four Great Tigers" moved from the village to teach in other places in China and around the world. Since nearly everyone was gone, and I knew someone needed to stay and keep up the level of practice in the village, I gave up the teaching post and returned to the hometown. Presently, my students are doing very well. I do not need to go see them compete anymore because I know how they will do.

Wang Xi'an and Cheng Jincai practicing
a counter to a joint-locking application.
(Plano, TX 5/2000)

■ I have noticed that lots of martial artists acknowledge taiji as a good health exercise but not as an effective martial art. Could you explain a bit about taiji training to help us understand more clearly?

Taiji training is very hard. You must train past your body's normal limits—many times past these normal limits. Normal training just will not do. You need to push. Back in Chen Village, all of the people were farmers. The winter and spring were not busy times, so we had a lot of time to practice. So I trained very hard through the summer heat and the winter cold. I had a long yard and I don't know how many times a day I would train the routines. Too many to count. If you want to make real improvement, it is important that you work past your normal limits.

Wang Xi'an practicing a movement from the
Chen-style's first routine—Shake Foot and Stretch
Down (Plano, TX, 5/2000); and from the second
routine—Wrap Fire Crackers (Paris, France 5/1994).

Even though we would have to lay off of training to do the seasonal farm work, we could retain our gongfu or cultivation. Just a few days of warming up and you would be very good again.

Training internal energy it is like the rain. When it is raining very hard, the water comes down very strong and is abundant. When it is not raining, the water evaporates and dries up. When you are training internal energy very well, you need to keep it going and growing. Do not stop too long and allow your internal energy cultivation to evaporate or recede. It is not like an underground spring in where you dig until you hit water and the water continues flowing forever. I used this analogy to clarify how you should train energy. If you want to build up very strong internal work, you must be consistent in practice and I reiterate that you must train many times beyond your normal limits.

As far as the martial aspect is concerned, most martial arts have special and secret methods. Chen-style also has methods that are unique and are not taught to the general public. Even I actually have methods that most taiji practitioners normally do not know.

The external martial styles are more straight in and straight out when it comes to punching and kicking. The internal styles emphasize more on breathing, mind control, and spiral movements. I feel that external styles are too demanding on the body. If practiced for too long, you will suffer when you get older. As the external martial artist ages, the bones and tendons start to show injury and then it is too late to really correct. If you only train "hard," the body is injured but you might not know it until it is too late.

Energy is generated from the inside and cultivated until it permeates the whole body from the most internal level to the surface of the skin. This makes you very healthy, but taiji is not just for that. It also builds very good fighting skills. External arts use explosive punching and kicking. The internal styles specialize in the use of spiral mechanics [chansijing], a unified way of delivering explosive power [fajing], as well as a way of dissipating power called yin jin luo kong. Yin jin luo kong means using your sensitivity to trick the opponent into attacking and then leading him into emptiness and then attacking him at his weakest moment. This is the internal arts usage of soft to fight hard. These are the high-level skills of taiji.

Wang Xi'an practicing a movement
from the Chen-style broadsword
Rolling Body Chopping (Paris, France, 5/1994).

Normally people watch taiji and ask, "How can that be used for fighting?" At this level, people are not really capable of understanding taiji's secrets. They only see the outside, yet have no feeling to complete the picture. Once they start training and start developing to a higher level, they say, "Oh, now I understand a little." This process repeats itself until the many little breakthroughs lead to real skills. Progress comes by gradually building up. You can't push people and make them understand this kind of thing.

The internal arts include weapons practice, but they are not really used for self-defense. In the old days, people used them for protection, but since then things have cooled off. Now the martial uses have become more secret. In older times, people trained real hard for protection. Now the emphasis has shifted more toward health. Currently, many people practice Yang Taijiquan because it was the first to reach the public eye and is easier to learn. People are likely to do it when they are only looking for health.

Chen-style is not only soft, it is also hard. It is not only slow, it is also fast. Yang-style leans toward the soft side and the Chen-style sticks to perfectly balancing the two extremes and is easily adjusted to all ages and body types. Chen-style is very flexible but always maintains the internal training. The difference is who can improve faster. If you want to improve faster, you need to work harder to reach a high level. Yang-style has internal training but soft training is not enough to reach high level or martial skill. If you want fighting skill, you will need special training.

First you build up internal energy from inside. You build up the whole body. The body becomes strong and internal energy can go through the whole body at the mind command. Then good fighting skill can be developed. Internal skills and health are developed at the same time. The special training for fighting skill requires in-depth knowledge of the applications of the Chen-style routines. Many people never reach this point in their training, so they never really understand about the fighting skills. That is the hard part of training.

■ [Li Shudong]: I once had a traditional martial arts teacher. If he did not know a student well, he would teach them motions but not usage. He wanted to keep the tradition of transmitting to the right people. He needed to know who really wanted to train, if they had good character and manners. He made sure everything was correct and only then he taught the secrets. These teachings are not easily divulged to the public, right?

No matter how much money people offer me, if they do not demonstrate the right character and I do not like teaching them, then no matter how much they pay, it won't matter. I would not teach them.

When it comes to martial skills, Chen-style has elements that the external styles have, such as numerous hitting, kicking, throwing, and joint locking techniques. Every style has those things. However, the spiral energy and short energy techniques, not everyone has those.

Taiji has five basic fighting skills: 1) feinting or dodging to trick an opponent, 2) grabbing techniques, 3) controlling, usually done with grabs and throws, 4) neutralizing attacks, and 5) hitting. These techniques are not isolated during usage. In fact, they are used together in various combinations according to the situation.

■ [Wang stands up to demonstrate a movement called "lazy about tying a robe." He then asks me to grab both of his wrists with all my strength. Suddenly he circles his waist, generating a tremendous shaking power, which throws me away and frees him from the double-handed grab. The power generated was both soft and powerful, at once generating such an immense jolt that I was slightly disoriented.]

I used this demonstration to show that not only do you have and use power, but you also use it very intelligently. You apply your power to just the right places that are the most vulnerable. Do not just hit the opponent. Sense the weakness in his power, then attack. In this case, the thumbs were the weak part of the hold so they were attacked to neutralize the hold.

When executing the movements of the form, every small detail needs to be articulated. The attention to these subtleties in the forms will determine your success in developing real taiji combative skills.

■ [Using the very beginning of the movement Lazy About Tying a Coat, he circles both hands upward and does a small pressing action by extending and settling the wrists to the front.]

This little pressing action at the top seems very small, but when it comes to martial technique, it is very important. You have this technique where the movement appears to be only neutralizing, but at the end there is a subtle attack hidden in the minute detail.

■ Could you please tell us of your experience with your teacher Chen Zhaopei?

Chen Zhaopei was a very good person. He did not have a chance to receive a high education, but his memory was incredible. He committed to memory most of the important aspects of Chinese history. In his younger days, he worked for the civil service. When he returned to Chen Village, he used all of his energy to help preserve Chen taiji. He would always try to answer every question a student had and watch their movements to try and understand what their problems were so that they could be corrected. He was extremely warmhearted. He would go way out of his way to teach and help people.

In 1972, the first competition was held in Dengfeng County, Henan Province. Chen Zhaopei was the head coach. By setting up formal classes and organizing competitions to promote development, he tried to build up Chen taiji from a secret family style to the level of a national art and sport.

I often had to attend meetings that would not end until late at night. After finishing my meetings, I would always stop by the school to find Chen Zhaopei inside with an oil lamp burning. So I would go see him and he would teach me a lot. Chen Zhaopei was quite fond of singing. He often sang in a traditional free-style type of singing in which the singer sings whatever is in his mind. Chen Zhaopei would often sing these lines:

> When I hear the rooster crow, I awake and practice taiji.
> Right now I am old, but I can still stick to the floor.
> I want someone who can be my successor.
> Even with sweat pouring out everywhere, I am quite happy.

■ What do you think about the level of taiji practice in the United States?

I am pleased to see the popularity of taiji rising in the U.S., but presently the Japanese display a higher level. This is due to the fact that they have been exposed to the top-level Chen masters for a longer time than the rest of the world outside of China. The higher-level Chen taiji has only been taught in the U.S. for a relatively short period. However, I am sure that the level will continue to rise in the next few years.

I am happy to see the rapid growth of taiji's popularity in such a short time. A lot of students are doing very well. However, I hope that they can practice more and for a longer time so that they can reach the deeper, more valuable aspects of taiji. I really appreciate the hospitality that everyone has shown me during this visit and I hope everyone gets a chance to visit Chen Village.

I have done a lot of traveling and teaching around the world and I have observed the constant rise in taiji's popularity. Right now I am trying to build up Chen Village because, although it is the seat of Chen-style, it is a very poor village. It does not have a lot of the amenities that foreign visitors are accustomed to. Some serious students do not care about those kinds of things, but it would help things out greatly if the living arrangements were a little more comfortable during their stay. Also, I have made sure that there are higher-level teachers there so that more people can stay and get the desired training. With all this in mind, I am in the process of building a large professional training facility with dormitories. This also will serve to support Chen villagers who are really interested in training professionally: they can live there while training.

Wang Xi'an practicing.
1) a transitional movement from the Chen-style's first routine—
Buddha's Warrior Attendant Pounds Mortar.
2) Chen-style's second routine—Elbow Hits the Heart.
3) Chen-style's first routine—Shake Foot and Stretch Down (Plano, TX 5/2000).

TECHNICAL SECTION

Chen taijiquan is packed with highly effective martial techniques ranging from simple to profound. Practitioners become competent at the Chen-style's repertoire of high-level fighting skills through the practice of forms, push-hands, fighting drills, stepping drills, and body conditioning. The following applications present an introduction to Chen taijiquan's arsenal. These applications provide examples of how some of Chen-style's basic skills and methods are integrated in practical combative applications.

Strategically, Chen-style uses defense as its offense, yet it is very flexible and adapts to any situation as needed. Chen-style practitioners generally do not struggle with or seek to overpower the opponent. Instead, the Chen stylist uses sensitivity developed from push-hands practice to find the path of least resistance and uses the opponent's force against them, adding his own power and body weight to the opponent's power. Techniques are crisply executed in a swift and fluid manner with precise timing, attacking an opponent at the weakest place at the most vulnerable time.

It should be noted that all of the essential concepts of Chen-style's numerous boxing skills are contained in the empty-hand and weapons forms. The applications featured in this article draw upon the following skills (Wallace, 1998: 58–89):

Eight boxing skills, also known as eight essential energies:
- ward off / resilient force
- roll back
- push
- press
- pluck
- split
- elbow strike, and
- leaning strike

The following technical section will illustrate the following:
- neutralization
- joint-locking
- spiral energy or silk-reeling
- return energy folding
- leading into emptiness
- striking
- stepping methods
- grabbing
- throwing
- kicking

Wallace, A. (1998). Internal training: The foundation for Chen Style Taijiquan's fighting skills and health promotion. *Journal of Asian Martial Arts*, 7(1): 58–89.

DEFENSE AGAINST A PUNCH
Skills Utilized: Neutralization of power, grab, and hit

1a The opponent punches at Cheng's face. He neutralizes the punch by sidestepping the attack while entering the opponent's space, blocking with his right hand without breaking the momentum of the punch.

1b Cheng quickly grabs the opponent's arm with his left hand then pulls the opponent into him, increasing the forward momentum of the punch. This literally sucks the opponent in and upsets his balance.

1c Cheng immediately punches to the side of the opponent's head. When applied at actual speed, the technique is executed in an instant and is very fluid utilizing sensitivity to fully capitalize upon the opponent's power.

TAKE DOWN
Skills Utilized: Return/Folding Energy

2a The opponent grabs Cheng's arms as if to grapple with him.

2b Cheng relaxes his shoulders and chest to neutralize the grabbing of his arms. He then inserts his left hand outside of the opponent's right arm and his right hand inside the opponent's left. Using the points of contact as the controlling point, Cheng fakes a throw to the right causing the opponent to resist.

2c As soon as the reflex to resist arises in the opponent, Cheng uses his looseness and sensitivity to suddenly fold to the left.

2d Fully capitalizing on the opponent's returning energy, Cheng forcefully slams the opponent to the ground.

JOINT LOCK
Skills Utilized: Pluck

3a The opponent punches to Cheng's face. Using the roll back technique, Cheng intercepts and deflects the punch with his left hand.

3b Cheng catches the elbow from the bottom with his right hand hooking his fingers in the crease of the elbow he then applies the plucking technique, twisting and folding the joints.

3c After he manipulates the opponent into a very awkward position he applies pressure to the locked joints generating great pain possibly dislocating the shoulder and seriously injuring the spine.

THROWING TECHNIQUE
Skills Utilized: Push (also translated as Crowding or Squeezing)

4a The opponent suddenly pushes Cheng's chest. Cheng immediately sinks down to stabilize his body.

4b He grabs the opponent's elbows and changes the angle of the elbow joints by rotating them outward. Cheng simultaneously expands his chest toward the opponent and pulls him in, generating the push or squeezing energy making the opponents arms collapse locking his wrists and causing his body over extend forward.

4c Cheng then explosively spirals his body and weight down to the right completely destroying the opponent's balance.

4d Cheng then forcefully flips the opponent over on to the ground.

KICK NEUTRALIZATION
Skills Utilized: Kicking Technique, Neutralization of Power
5a   Cheng and the opponent square off.

5b   The opponent delivers a front kick. Cheng rotates his body to the right, neutralizing the kick. He then catches the kick from the bottom.

5c-d Cheng completes the catching of the kick with his left hand locking the knee. He then delivers a side heel kick to the inside of the knee, which takes the opponent down, possibly dislocating or breaking the knee.

JOINT LOCK
Skills Utilized: Pluck
6a   The opponent grabs Cheng's wrist.

6b   Cheng rotates his arm clockwise exploiting the range of motion of the opponent's arm and then grabs the opponent's wrist before he can let go.

6c   Cheng then sinks his body and opens his arm forward, generating immense pressure on the opponent's already locked wrist and forearm and setting him up to be hit in the face.

TAKE DOWN
Skills Utilized: Press, leading into emptiness

7a The opponent forcefully pushes Cheng's chest.

7b Cheng sinks his body and loosens his joints allowing the opponent's force to be conducted to the ground without toppling him. Cheng simultaneously places his hands on top of the opponent's forearms.

7c He then relaxes and hollows his chest while pressing downward on the opponent's incoming force. This causes the opponent to suddenly fall into emptiness.

7d As the opponent falls in, Cheng adds his own force pressing downward, slamming the opponent to the ground.

THROW
Skill Utilized: Joint Locking

8a The opponent grabs Cheng's arms as if to grapple with him.

8b Cheng then grabs inside the opponent's right elbow with his left hand and outside the left elbow with his right hand. He twists the right elbow inside, locking the joints on the right while pressing the outside of the left elbow causing the opponent to fold to the right.

8c Cheng then drops his body weight while explosively spiraling the hips down to the left, forcefully slamming the opponent to the ground.

JOINT LOCK
Skills Utilized: Pluck

9a The opponent punches at Cheng's face. Cheng rotates his body out of the way and catches the opponent's wrist and elbow.

9b He then guides the opponent's elbow into the fold of his own elbow to stabilize the elbow while folding the wrist to create a very firm joint lock.

9c Cheng then applies pressure to the locked joints generating immense pain at the wrist allowing him to manipulate the opponent into a very vulnerable position and strike him or severely damage the tissues in the wrist.

Wang Xi'an practicing a movement
from the Chen-style straight sword
routine called Immortal Points
the Way (Plano, TX 5/2000).

NAMES OF PEOPLE

Chen Fake	陳發科
Chen Zhaokuai	陳照奎
Wang Xian	王西安
Chen Xiaowang	陳小旺
Chen Zhenglei	陳正雷
Zhu Tiancai	朱天才
Cheng Jincai	程進才
Li Shudong	李樹東

* Special thanks goes to Li Shudong for helping with the translation while conducting this interview.

A Brief Description of
Chen-Style Master Du Yuze

by Wong Jiaxiang
Introduction and Translation
by Michael A DeMarco

17th Generation Chen-style Master Du Yuze.
Photograph, provided by Tu Zongren, taken in
Du's Taipei living room during the mid-1970's.

Introduction

The following translation is an excerpt from *Master Du Yuze's Eighty-Second Birthday Commemorative Book*, originally written by Wang Jiaxiang. I have chosen to translate part of this booklet for a number of reasons. One reason was to commemorate the 94th birthday Master Du had in 1989.

Regardless of age, Master Du was certainly a unique figure in the world of martial arts. Boxing instructors of various styles acknowledge Du Yuze's unique mastery of the Chen system, believing it to be a national treasure. Instructor Adam Hsu, now teaching in the San Francisco area, compared many Chen-styles while in China in 1986. Hsu, previously from Taiwan, wrote in a correspondence that "Du's Chen-style is indeed a national treasure. Even in Chen Village, the birthplace of taijiquan, you find almost no one teaching Chen-style like this."

Along with Du Yuze's unique place in the lineage of Chen-style masters, his personal history is likewise quite interesting. Master Du began his martial art training at an early age partly because of his father's high social standing as a government official. During the later years of the Qing Dynasty (1644–191 1), when the political and social conditions were not stable, such a position necessitated the need for bodyguards. The Du family lived under constant guard and visitors to their home were limited to close friends, those who had business with Du's father, or hired instructors.

Because of the above conditions, young Du Yuze was able to study with two great teachers: Masters Chen Yanxi and Chen Mingbiao. Under their guidance he learned both the old form (*laojia*) and new form (*xinjia*) sets of the Chen system. Oddly enough, because of the strict household formalities, Master Du never met Chen Fake, the son of Chen Yanxi. Incidently, Chen Fake created the new form, based on the two routines of laojia (the second known as Cannon First, or *Paochui*).

A word regarding Wang Jiaxiang will help explain his interest and insights in writing the Commemorative Book. Mr. Wang, along with Mr. Tu Zongren, Mr. Li Houcheng and Mr. Cao Delin represent the four formal students who have performed the traditional ceremony of kowtowing to Master Du. As a result, they were accepted as "sons" within the Chen taijiquan family and are numbered as "sons" in that order. This continues the lineage of Chen Yanxi, since Du Yuze was one of his accepted "sons." Mr. Wang Jiaxiang is now nearly seventy years old and continues to teach in the southern Taiwan city of Tainan.

The following translation of his "Brief Description of Master Du Yuze" I hope will provide interesting details in the tradition of a boxing master. Hopefully it will also indicate the deep feeling and dedication necessary to transform the movements into a perfected art form. Those who have been fortunate enough to fall under the tutelage and inspiration of respected Master Du have also accepted the responsibility to pass on the learning in like manner.

Except where noted, the accompanying photographs were taken at Master Du's home on June 8, 1989, while the "sons" of Mr. Tu Zongren were there to receive some additional instruction. Master Du, carefully watching every movement of the students, spoke in a strong clear voice (in Chinese, English or German!) to make critical remarks. When words were of no use, he stood to demonstrate. His gongfu was certainly impressive as was his kind personality which radiated the wisdom of his years. This combination of gentleman and master made Du Yuze an indubitably rare form of dragon.

Du Yuze (age 94).
Photo taken June 8, 1989,
at is home in Taipei.

116

Below: Sword practice. Photos, provided
by Wong Jiaxiang, show Du Yuze in
the years prior to his move to Taiwan.

Translation*

Master Du Yuze, whose secondary given name is Du Qimin, was from Henan Province, Boai prefecture. He was born in the twenty-third year of the Qing Dynasty's Emperor Guangxu; in other words, fifteen years before the 1911 founding of the Chinese Republic, between 5:00 and 7:00 p.m.

Now he is more than eighty-two years old and still practices taijiquan regularly. This practice includes Golden Buddha Pounds Pestle, 1,000 Pounds Fall, Shake Foundation and Kick Twice, Concealed-hand Strike, Strike Towards Groin, Stop Opponent with One Heel (left and right), Swing Foot to Double Target, steps, vertical movements, jumps, leaps… He practices every kind of movement, clearly and crisply, placing all in good order. The result is a boxing borne on the wind. At the same time, he has achieved great strength and the briskness of sound health. Because Master Du does not give up this practice, he has remained at his prime. Ah! If one can do all of taiji's profound functions, it is possible to make great progress!

In the eighth year of the Chinese Republican period, when the country was finally stabilized (following great political unrest), Du Yuze attended college to study mechanical engineering. Following his studies, he performed engineering duties in the region of northern China. Afterwards, he came to Taiwan and was employed as an engineering specialist and worked secondarily as a factory manager. Passing through these years in this way was a rewarding experience.

Master Du was originally from Henan, Boai prefecture. Chenjiagou, located in Wen prefecture, is less than seventeen miles away. In the late Qing Dynasty, these same areas formed part of what was then the district of Huaiqing prefecture. This rural area had a close-knit society where everybody knew everyone else who lived there.

When he was eighteen years old, Du Yuze kowtowed to Master Chen Yanxi as part of his formal acceptance as a student. Chen Yanxi was the famed sixteenth generation master of the Chen-style and grandson of Chen Changxing. Chen Yen-xi taught Du Yuze the *laojia* (old form) Chen family system.

The father of Du Yuze was named Du Yomei. Thirty years before the Qing Emperor Guangxu (reign lasted from 1875 to 1908), Du Yomei had the rare fortune of passing the Jinshi Examination (national civil service examination held at the capital) and was awarded the eleventh degree, the second most outstanding rank that could be received from the Hanlin Academy (government examination office). Du Yomei went abroad to study in Japan during the early Republican years (1912–1949). While in government service, he also traveled to the provinces of Guandong and Guanxi.

Du Yomei asked Chen Yanxi's nephew, Chen Mingbiao, to be his bodyguard, plus his family's personal boxing teacher. He did so because Chen Mingbiao was an expert in archery, the spear and other aspects of the martial arts, including the *xinjia* (new form) Chen family taiji and Paochui (Cannon Fist). Consequently, Du Yuze was able to study the xinjia and Paochui styles under his tutelage.

The movements of the Chen Village style of taijiquan are organized in a series, bound together as by a strong silk thread. To elaborate further, the movements are alternating manifestations of fast and slow; varying degrees of hard and soft as well as varying degrees of empty and substantial.

How to execute these principles in their highest degree is a precious secret not easily shown to others, particularly in an agricultural society whose people must work so much while they study. Therefore, the transmission of this knowledge has not been broad. In Taiwan, those who have received training in Chen-style taijiquan are as rare as the mythical phoenix or unicorn. In the past, anyone who could perform the Chen-style learned it, like Master Du, during the Qing Dynasty. Because of Master Du's deep commitment to this particular boxing art, he feels a great obligation to preserve what he learned. He repeatedly made appeals to others in Taiwan to follow this path. Master Du, desiring not to neglect this duty to pass on his knowledge, teaches as much as possible by demonstration, so later generations can advance accordingly.

At present, taijiquan is flourishing as a fruit from its roots in Chenjiagou, the village in Wen prefecture of Henan province. And yet, just how to do the Chen-style taijiquan remains a secret. In addition, the excessive secrecy that surrounds it has placed the art on the verge of extinction. The sixteenth generation Master Chen Pinsan, by giving his total attention for thirteen years, collected, structured, organized and eventually published what he could find regarding taijiquan, including pictures, diagrams and stories.

In the preface at the beginning of this book is a remark that Master Du shares with the respected taijiquan elders: "Indications show that efforts are being made to examine and cultivate the principles of yin and yang in equal fashion." This is being done in order to incorporate the theory of the epigram into the performance of taijiquan and thus bring the art to its full realization. But to research, study and actually acquire this special skill requires guidance.

Together with our upcoming generations, we all have to share the responsibility of seeing that Chen taijiquan can continue to flourish forever without interruption.

Taiwan, Sixty-Third Year of the Republic of China (1974)
Chrysanthemum Month (ninth lunar month)
Respectfully your student, Wang Jiaxiang

* For clarification, the translator has placed additional information within parentheses. Any imperfections in this translation are solely due to the limited linguistic skills of the translator.

Master Du's adopted sons (*tudi*), standing behind him for a photograph taken on his 80th birthday. Although he instructed other students, only these four were selected to be "sons," thus inheriting the most significant details of his teachings. Standing, left to right: Wang Jiaxiang 王嘉祥, Li Houcheng 李後成, Cao Delin 曹德鄰, Tu Zongren 凃宗仁. *Photo provided by Tu Zongren.*

Above: On the grounds of Sun Yatsen Memorial Hall, near his home, Du Yuze posed for photos. He was nearly 80 years old at the time. *Photo provided by Chong Jiensiong.*

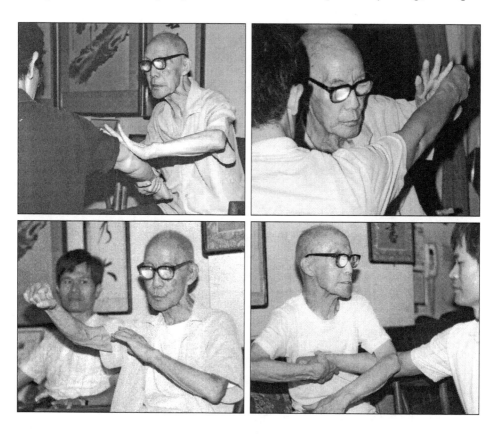

Above: Du Yuze demonstrating applications. Master Du removes his shirt to more freely demonstrate movements. Here he shows some defensive blocks, grabs and counter strikes while stressing the application of each according to the yin/yang principles of taiji. Even at 94 years of age, Master Du did not hesitate to stand in order to perform movements when talk alone was insufficient. Many of the profound aspects of taijiquan are beyond words.

Above, left: Dietmar Stubenbaum receives precious advice from Master Du. After students performed techniques, Du would analyze each movement, usually mixing Daoist theory with varied martial applications. He lamented that many martial arts are losing aspects of their rich heritage. According to him, it was after the introduction of firearms that teachings became more limited in scope. Right: Some photos accompanying this text were taken the day Dietmar Stubenbaum, Michael DeMarco, and Huang Shichuan partook in the ritual for discipleship. Here DeMarco kowtows three times in front of Master Du as part of the ritual.

Below: Du's taiji family extends: At center is Master Du with Tu Zongren to his left. Back row, left to right: Dietmar Stubenbaum, Michael DeMarco, and Huang Shichuan.

Master Wang Jiaxiang 王嘉祥

Above left: Now a major representative of the eighteenth generation Chen taijiquan masters, Wang is one of the most knowledgeable practitioners of the style living today. Originally from the far northeastern province of Heilungjiang, he now resides in Tainan city, Taiwan. Above right: Mr. Wong practicing a movement from the first routine in which the performer "drops and branches," springing back up immediately into the next movement. *Photos provided by Wong Jiaxiang.*

Passing of Grandmaster Du

On March 16, 1990, Du Yuze peacefully passed away in Taipei Veteran's Hospital at 10:30a.m.

ABRIDGED LINEAGE CHART
Chen Yanxi (陳延熙) & Chen Mingbiao (陳名標)

↓

Du Yuze (杜毓澤)
17th generation (1886–1990).
From Baoi, Henan; approximately 17 miles from Chen Village.

↓

18th generation disciples according to seniority from left to right:

Wang Jiaxiang	**Tu Zongren**	**Li Houcheng**	**Cao Delin**
b. 1925	b. 1944	b. 1936 – d. 1984	b. 1925
lives in Tainan.	lives in Taipei.	lived in Taipei.	Lives in Chiyi.

19th generation disciples according to seniority from top to bottom:

Lee Chengchong b. 1946 Lives in Chongli. Tsai Yingchien b. 1947 Lives in Kaohsiung. Ho Hongtsai b. 1952 Lives in Pingtong. Lin Chongpor b. 1954 Lives in Taipei. Chang Chourjinn b. 1954 Lives in Chiayi. Chong Khensiong b. 1956 Lives in Tainan. Chou Mingfa b. 1958; Lives in Tainan. Chiang Dingfung b. 1961. Lives in Tainan. Hwang Shiang b. 1963. Lives in Tainan.	Michael A. DeMarco b. 1953 Lives in Erie, PA., USA. Huang Shirchuan b. 1952 Lives in Taipei. Dietmar Stubenbaum b. 1962 Lives in Friedrichshafen, Germany. Lin Shirchien b. 1951 Lives in Taipei. You Jindi b. 1952 Lives in Taipei.	Li Yincun b. 1972 in Taipei. Li Houcheng's son.	Suan Shufeng b. 1953 Female disciple Lives in Chiyi.

index

Made in the USA
Charleston, SC
28 August 2015